BUFFOONS, QUEENS
and
WOODEN HORSEMEN

BUFFOONS, QUEENS
and
WOODEN HORSEMEN

The Dyo and Gouan Societies
of the Bambara of Mali

by

PASCAL JAMES IMPERATO

With a Foreword by
Irwin Hersey

1983
KILIMA HOUSE PUBLISHERS
NEW YORK

Library of Congress Catalog Card Number 82-82902
ISBN 0-910385-00-9

Printed in the United States of America

Typeset by Diane Lubarsky and Book Design by Chaia Lehrer

Produced at The Print Center, Inc., Box 1050, Brooklyn, N.Y., 11202, a non-profit printing facility for literary and arts-related publications. Funded by The New York State Council on the Arts and the National Endowment for the Arts.

This Book
Is
Dedicated
To The Memory of
LOUISE ARLETTE OCTAVIE DELAFOSSE
(1910-1982)

CONTENTS

BUFFOONS, QUEENS
and
WOODEN HORSEMEN

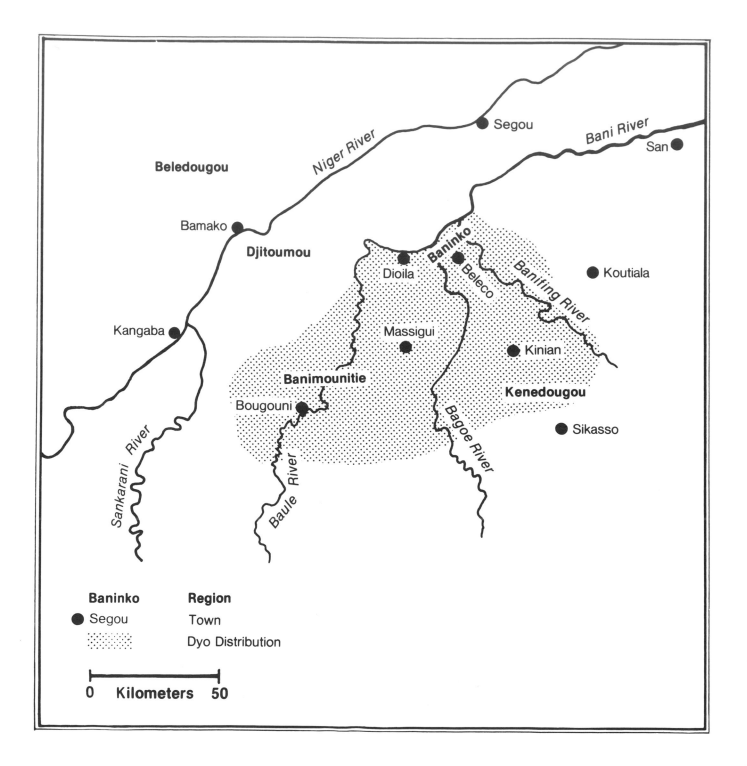

Beledougou

Niger River

Segou

Bani River

San

Bamako

Djitoumou

Baninko

Dioila

Beleco

Banifing River

Koutiala

Kangaba

Massigui

Kinian

Banimounitie

Kenedougou

Bougouni

Sikasso

Sankarani River

Baule River

Bagoe River

Baninko   **Region**

● Segou   Town

⋮⋮⋮⋮   Dyo Distribution

0   **Kilometers**   50

Foreword

This is an important book because it focuses attention on an area, people and secret societies about which virtually nothing was known until the 1950's, and, perhaps even more important, about which much that has been published in the intervening years has been either erroneous or incomplete.

As the author notes in his introduction, anthropologists and ethnographers have had a tendency to regard the Bambara as a homogeneous people, with the same or similar religious and cultural institutions, but this is simply not so, particularly in the case of the southern Bambara, with which this study deals.

The southern Bambara, existing in an area far removed from Kaarta and Segou, the principal centers of Bambara religion and culture, and subject to the influences of many neighboring peoples with quite different religions and cultures, have developed secret societies such as the *Dyo* and *Gouan* which are markedly different from the much better-known Bambara societies, like the *Tyi Wara, N'Tomo, Komo, Kwore* and *Kono.*

So different, in fact, are some of the objects produced for *Dyo* and *Gouan* rituals that for many years whole categories of objects were regarded as being fake, or late, or made for sale to tourists, because they simply didn't fit into what was then regarded as the normal Bambara mode.

This fine work will help correct that erroneous impression. It is an important contribution because it has become quite obvious, down through the years, as more and better research has been done on traditional African religion and culture, that there is far less homogeneity among the people of Africa than was previously thought.

This is particularly true when one closely examines traditional African artifacts. It is striking to learn, when one does this, that so few African sculptures are "pure" anything. Instead, one finds many more objects which are clearly mixtures of various cultural influences, such as Bambara and Dogon, for example, or Bambara and Senufo, in this particular geographic area.

Thus, this study will be of interest both to scholars and collectors. To scholars, because it provides a full-scale examination of two southern Bambara societies about which very little has previously been written. And to collectors, because it provides them with an opportunity to learn that objects which until now have been suspect are in actuality authentic.

The author, while not a trained anthropologist or ethnographer, is a member of a group which has made major contributions to both these fields—the enlightened amateur. He is particuarly fortunate in that he had scientific training, which permits him to avoid some of the pitfalls into which other amateurs have fallen.

He is perhaps most fortunate in the fact his vocation as an internationally known and respected specialist in tropical medicine has provided him with so many opportunities to pursue his avocation of anthropology.

This study is therefore not just another armchair analysis, but instead is based on almost six years of intensive fieldwork in Mali among the very people and institutions about which he is now writing. In addition, as a trained scientist, he had the ability to judge the veracity of what was told to him by his informants.

Buffoons, Queens and Wooden Horsemen is thus an important work, not only for what it has to tell us specifically about the southern Bambara, the *Dyo* and *Gouan* societies, and the artifacts used in the rituals of these societies, but also for what it implies about important cultures in many other parts of Africa.

It is to be hoped that future years will see the publication of additional studies of this region by Dr. Imperato.

November 24th, 1982

Irwin Hersey
Editor and Publisher
PRIMITIVE ART NEWSLETTER

Introduction

The Bambara, comprising some two and a half million people, are the largest ethnic group in Mali. They are sedentary agriculturists who live primarily in an inverted triangular area in west central Mali covering 400,000 square miles of flat savanna. They hold a dominant political, social, and economic position in modern Mali, and their language, *Bamanan-kan*, is the lingua franca in much of the country. Also known as the Bamana, the Bambara belong to the great Manding family of peoples. The term Manding is used to cover a number of West African groups who share a similar culture and who speak related forms of the same language. The three most important Manding groups are the Bambara, the Malinke (Maninka) who live west of the Bambara in Mali and in Guinea, Gambia, and Senegal, and the Dyula who are a merchant group living south of the Bambara in Mali and the Ivory coast. The Malinke number about 800,000 and the Dyula about 600,000.

Many of the Bambara, including their caste of Somono fishermen on the Niger, look to Segou and Kaarta as their cultural centers rather than to the Manding heartland since these were the important centers of the Bambara kingdoms of the 17th and 18th centuries. Over the last century and more especially in the past few decades, Islam has been gradually spreading among these people. But many of them are still animist, remaining faithful to their ancient religion. The Bambara are primarily agriculturists, but those living in the central and nothern regions keep sizeable herds of cattle, sheep, and goats. They live in villages that vary in size from 100 or so inhabitants to over 1,000, the average village having about 500 inhabitants. Through their conquests, the Bambara carried the Manding language as far north as Timbuctoo and Mauritania and eastward into the heart of the inland delta of the Niger. The Bambara form of the Manding language was used by the French colonial administration as a *lingua franca* and they carried it throughout West Africa.[1]

The Bambara are farmers who grow millet, corn, and manioc and who keep small herds of goats, sheep, and cattle. They are polygamous, patriarchal, patrilineal and patrilocal. Marriage involves a bride price paid to the parents of the bride. This consists of clothing, textiles, cattle, and in recent years cash payments.

According to tradition, the Bambara arrived on the banks of th Middle Niger near the present town of Segou in the early 17th century.[2] The Soninke, descendants of the Ghana Empire, were living there at the time. In 1712, Mamari Coulibaly, known as Biton Coulibaly, founded a kingdom around the town of Segou. He became the *fama* (king) of what was to develop into a powerful political state. To the northwest, another powerful Bambara chief, Sey Bamana, established a kingdom, known as the Kaarta Kingdom.

Biton Coulibaly gradually conquered a huge area around Segou, and administratively and militarily organized his state in an admirable manner. He formed the *ton-dyon*, a special standing army which started as a royal guard composed of captured enemy soldiers and slaves. He extended the borders of Segou northeastward to Djenne and drove the enemy Massasi Bambara into Kaarta where they formed a separate kingdom of their own. When he died from tetanus in 1755, he was succeeded by his sons, both of whom were killed by the *ton-dyon*. They then made one of their own members king. In 1760, N'Golo Diarra, a *ton-dyon* was made king. He ruled until 1787 and became Segou's greatest king and founder of the Diarra dynasty which lasted until 1862.[3] He conquered the Peul, and the cities of Djenne and Timbuctoo. When he died in 1787, his son Monson became king (1787-1808). After his reign the kingdom began to decline. In 1862, Segou fell to the Moslem Tukulor warrior, El Hadj Omar Tall, and in 1864 his son, Amadou Tall, became the king of Segou until 1892 when the French drove him out.[4]

The Bambara kings were in effect priest-kings, because they headed the state religion and presided over all of its cults. When the

Tukulor conquered the Bambara, they attempted to impose Islam by force. Although the Bambara kings were not Moslem (except for Ali, one of Biton Coulibaly's sons, who was murdered by the *ton-dyon*), they tolerated the Moslem Soninke people in their midst. The latter were vital to the trade of the kingdom and were Segou's main means of commercial exchange with Timbuctoo, North Africa, and the coast. The Tukulor were officially intolerant of the Bambara religion in both Segou and Kaarta, but were unsuccessful in completely destroying it. However, they did have a major negative impact on the public manifestations of the Bambara religion, particularly in large towns and trading centers.

The Kaarta Kingdom of the Bambara never achieved the administrative and political cohesion of its sister kingdom of Segou. Its last king was put to death by El Hadj Omar Tall in 1854 when he captured the capital of Nioro.

Between Kaarta and Segou lies a large area known as the Beledougou. Neither Segou nor Kaarta were ever able to bring this area under their control, nor were the Tukulor successful in conquering it. Composed of small powerful chiefdoms which united as required against a common cause, the Beledougou preserved its ancient traditions and the traditional Bambara religion better than any of the other Bambara areas.

Another region, the Baninko (land beyond the Bani), that lies to the southwest of Segou, was frequently in a state of revolt against the Tukulor. But it lacked the political cohesion that made resistance in Beledougou so successful. Nonetheless, this region and adjacent areas resisted the influences of Islam well into the present century. Thus the traditional Bambara religion as locally practiced and a number of cultural institutions thrived there until even the 1970's.

It is tempting to view the pre-Islamic Bambara as a homogeneous people, possessing common social, political, cultural and religious institutions and a common history. But this is not the case. The Bambara are in effect a collection of similar peoples, who share common traditions, but who also manifest

striking local divergences in speech, culture and religious beliefs. These differences are especially marked in the southern Bambara country, whose people have been exposed to cultural influences emanating from such adjacent peoples as the Senufo, Minianka, Bobo and Wasalu. Coupled with these influences has been the effect of distance from the main centers of Bambara culture and religion, Kaarta and Segou. From a certain perspective, one can view the pre-Islamic cultural institutions and religion of this southern area as primordial, out of which the Bambara elaborated the complex religious and cultural institutions once characteristic of pre-Tukulor Segou. But there is also cogency in the argument that both regions simultaneously developed different, but in some ways similar religious and cultural institutions. Finally, there is the possibility that the southern Bambara retained only summary institutions, derived from the more complicated ones retained by their northern neighbors. Whatever the dynamics of development, the cultural and religious societies of the southern Bambara markedly differed from those of other Bambara groups. While these other Bambara groups possessed a highly structured system of initiation societies that included the *N'Tomo, Kwore, Komo, Kono, Nama* and *Tyi Wara*, many of the southern Bambara did not. Their *Dyo* society, consisting of several groups, some with both male and female memberships, encompassed many of the functions of the *Komo, Tyi Wara, Kwore* and *Nama*. And their *Gouan* society, that admitted both men and women, strongly focused on women's concerns. Closely linked to the *Dyo*, and indeed viewed as part of it in some areas, the *Gouan* was essentially a sodality in which women occupied leadership positions.

The first detailed study of the structure and functions of the *Dyo* was published in 1954 by professor Viviana Paques.[5] The *Gouan* society, however, was not even mentioned in the anthropological literature on the Bambara until 1974.[6] Prior to that time its art forms, particularly large wooden sculptures of seated women, remained very much of an enigma. Although these statues had first come into western collections in sizeable numbers in the 1950's, a period when the society was rapidly disintegrating, virtually nothing was known about them until 1974.

The focus of this book is on the art forms of both the *Dyo* and *Gouan* societies. Relevant sociologic and religious topics are discussed in sufficient detail to provide some idea of the contexts in which these objects were once used. The new information presented was gathered in the field during five years of continuous residence in Mali, extending from December 1966 through November 1971. During that time my primary responsibilities were to eradicate smallpox and control measles in Mali and develop the country's mobile medical services under the auspices of the United States Public Health Service and the United States Agency for International Development. By definition, these efforts required my spending long periods of time traveling in the bush, supervising the work of as many as twenty mobile teams of vaccinators and nurses. Because of the sudden appearance of cholera, never before known in Mali, and the re-emergence of yellow fever, I had to undertake other mobile vaccination campaigns throughout the country as well. In 1972, 1973 and 1974, I made three return visits to Mali, covering a five month period. The main purposes of my visits were to design immediate medical and relief programs for the victims of the sahelian drought and to develop long term programs for strengthening Mali's health care infrastructure. However, during these return visits I was able to add to the information I had previously gathered about the *Dyo* and *Gouan* societies.

The inquiries upon which this book is based were conducted over a very wide area of the southern Bambara country. This included the Bainimounitie, Baninko and Kenedougou, regions that are primarily in the modern administrative cercles of Bougouni, Dioila, Sikasso, Koutiala and Bla. Inquiries were also conducted in Kolokani.

In 1974, when I completed my field studies of the *Dyo* and *Gouan* societies, I assumed a highly demanding office in New York City, specifically that of First Deputy

Commissioner of Health. In 1977 and 1978 I served as Commissioner of Health of New York City and Chairman of the Board of Directors of the New York City Health and Hospitals Corporation and subsequently as Professor and Chairman of the Department of Preventive Medicine and Community Health at the State University of New York, Downstate Medical Center. The professional obligations of these positions left me little time for writing up the numerous field studies I had conducted of Bambara and Dogon art. Thus I had to publish my research over an extended period of time. My field studies of the *Dyo* and *Gouan* societies and their art forms were extensive and this coupled to the paucity of time available to me for writing on African art resulted in a preparation period of several years.

During the latter part of the 1970's, the need for this publication became acutely evident. A prodigious number of catalogues and books were published on African art during this period. Many of them consistently gave validity to what had originally been educated guesses about many *Dyo* and *Gouan* sculptures or else identified them by such unhelpful terms as fertility statue, maternity figure, ritual iron and the like. Surprisingly, many of those who authored these catalogues and books did not bother to draw upon the information that was already available, perhaps because it was scant and present in hard to find sources. It is my earnest hope that the information contained in this publication will be of help to scholars and collectors alike.

A large number of people made this publication possible. Although the *Dyo* and *Gouan* societies had largely ceased to function publicly, many people still continued to conduct residuary private rites. The secret nature of these societies require that many of my informants remain anonymous.

I am especially grateful to N'Tyi Kolekele, Brahima Malle, Gassou Fall, Moussa Kante, Djadouga Fane, Modibo Keita, Amadou Sanogo and Djigui Diakite who greatly facilitated my field research. I also want to thank the numerous villagers in the Baule and Bague river valleys whose hospitality and assistance greatly facilitated not only this study, but also the medical work I undertook at the same time.

The late Louise Delafosse, daughter of the late Maurice Delafosse, was a great source of encouragement and support to me in my work. I regret that she is not here to see this publication.

I want to thank Professor Viviana Paques of the University of Strasbourg for generously permitting me to reproduce her field photographs of the *Dyo* society. I am also grateful to her for reading an early draft of the manuscript. My sincere thanks go to Professor Dominique Zahan of the Sorbonne for reading the manuscript and for his helpful comments. His counsel and wisdom have been of great assistance to me over the past twelve years in my studies of Bambara art. I owe a great debt of gratitude to my wife Eleanor who in addition to raising two small children and developing her career found the time to read several revisions of the manuscript and help me in photographing many of the objects depicted in this book. I am grateful to Marli Shamir for her permission to reproduce photographs she made of *Dyo* sculpture from my collection when we both lived in Mali. The late Eliot Elisofon taught me the basic skills for photographing sculpture in natural sunlight during the several periods when he was my house guest in Mali. I am grateful to Franka and Viktor Kurti of TLC Photographic Laboratories in New York City for their advice on photographing sculptures in artificial light and for developing and printing many of the photographs shown here. And finally I would like to thank Mr. Alan Chapman and the staff of the Goldwater Memorial Library, the Metropolitan Museum of Art, for their helpful assistance and the museum for permission to reproduce photographs of objects in the Michael C. Rockefeller Memorial Collection.

Chapter 1

Recent *Dyow* History

The Bambara once possessed a number of initiation societies or associations, six of which were widespread and others which were confined to specific regions. These associations are collectively referred to as *dyow* (*dyo*-singular.) The word *dyo* means "slave," an appropriate term since members were perceived as being liberated after periods of rigorous initiation. The six major *dyow* have been described by several scholars, although the amount of information about each varies considerably.

The *N'Tomo* and the *Kwore* have been exhaustively described by Zahan and the *Komo* by a number of authors.[1-7] The *Tyi Wara* has been carefully documented by Imperato and Zahan and the *Nama* commented on by Monteil, Tauxier and de Zeltner.[8-12] The *Kono*, while mentioned by a number of scholars, has not been described in any great detail by those who observed it while it still functioned.

The six major *dyow* just mentioned generally restricted membership to men and were widely distributed throughout the Bambara country. However, there were and still are a number of *dyow* for women, whose geographic distribution is much more limited. Over three quarters of a century ago, Henry observed the *Mousso Ka Dyiri* association for women in the southeastern Bambara country.[13] In the 1950's Paques, who worked in the western and central regions, mentioned three such *dyow*, *Niagua*, *Kulukuto* and *Dyide*.[14] More recently some of the women's *dyow* have been described in greater detail as they relate to health and medical care.[15]

In addition to these *dyow* there were others that were of local importance. Two of these, which are the focus of this presentation, were the *Dyo* and the *Gouan*. They once flourished in the southern Bambara country, remaining functional until the 1960's. Of great significance is the fact that women were admitted to both of these societies. As is the case with most of the other *dyow*, they are now virtually extinct. To understand these associations and the representational art objects once used in their ceremonies and rituals requires some background knowledge of the *dyow* in general.

McNaughton cogently defines the *dyow* as religious, political, judicial and philosophical associations whose chief aim was the maintenance of social, spiritual and economic harmony.[16] Zahan has described the *N'Tomo, Komo, Nama, Kono, Tyi Wara* and *Kwore* as links in a chain that led to the progressive acquisition of wisdom and knowledge. The focus of each *dyow* was on an important aspect of human endeavor. Additionally, initiation exposed members to an enormous corpus of information dealing with the Bambara world view and man's role in the universal order. Thus each association and all of them in concert served as powerful instruments for the maintenance of social control, law and order. The *N'Tomo* was in a sense the prefatory association through which the noncircumcised were initiated into the *Komo* which acted as a village and even regional police force, punishing murderers, thieves, debtors and sorcerers. The *Nama* was an antisorcery association and the *Kono* a complimentary association to the *Komo* through which all human activity was monitored by means of omnipresent powers. The *Tyi Wara*, the least secretive of the *dyow*, in the sense that women and children were permitted to witness its public rituals, was concerned with agriculture. The *Kwore* was the highest level of initiation in many areas of the Bambara country, consisting of multiple hierarchical levels, passage through which brought man into union with the creator and enabled him to conquer death through reincarnation. The public manifestations of the *Kwore* were impressive and dramatic. Particularly well remembered are the performances of the *Kwore Duga*, masked buffoons who rode hobby horses and dressed in a manner that was simultaneously absurd and obscene. Zahan has splendidly assessed these performances as an attempt to depict life as ridiculous and as a device for prompting *Kwore* members to rise above the banalities of life to man's spiritual level of existence.[17]

Decline of The *Dyow*

Prior to the arrival of French colonial rule, many of these societies had been influenced by Islam to some degree. Until the mid-nineteenth century, Islam was more often than not a gentle insinuating force whose agents were long distance Moslem merchants traveling the trade routes that emanated out of Timbuctoo, Djenne and the coastal entrepots. In addition, neighboring Islamic states such as the Peul Empire of Macina made overt efforts to convert the animist Bambara. But all of this dramatically changed in the 1850's. At that time, fanatical Moslem warriors under the leadership of the Tukulor, El Hadj Omar, swept eastward in a *jihad* out of the Fouta Toro of Senegal and across most of the Bambara country. In 1854 they conquered the Massasi Bambara kingdom of Kaarta and in 1861 entered the capital of Segou. For almost forty years, the Tukulor attempted to impose a theocratic Moslem hegemony over the Bambara. They were constantly beset by open revolt which they met with a brutal force well documented by French explorers who witnessed it.[18] Their rule, well remembered by the Bambara today, was characterized by mass executions, the destruction of the external manifestations of the Bambara religion, including shrines, masks and idols and the imposition of obligatory Moslem practices on the Bambara leadership. Bambara chiefs were forced to shave their heads, abstain from alcohol and the eating of dog and horse meat, keep only four wives and publicly pray.[19]

These and other measures were actively enforced through intimidation, persuasion and physical force by a complex network of Tukulor administrators and a standing army. They were sustained in some parts of the Bambara country for close to four decades, the span of two generations at that time, and

were successful in erasing many of the external elements of the *dyow*. Thus by the time the French arrived and established colonial rule in the 1980's, the *dyow* had either disappeared or undergone substantial changes in many areas of the Bambara country.

Tauxier provides a vivid anecdotal account of what the Tukulor did when confronted with the *Komo*. This account was given by an eyewitness. Two masked *Komo* dancers, dressed in straw were behind a village with the members of the association when four hundred Tukulor horsemen arrived. The Tukulor leader rhetorically asked what these beings were and answered that surely they were not men. He then ordered that they be set on fire to see what they were. The camouflaged *Komo* dancers took off their costumes and pleaded that they were indeed men. The Tukulor then seized them and sold them as slaves at a nearby market.[20] Tauxier also relates that a Tukulor soldier was staying overnight in a Bambara village when the *Komo* was scheduled to emerge. As a non-initiate he was advised by his host to remain indoors. Instead he waited for the masked dancer on the line of march and when menaced by him shot him in the legs. The dancer fell to the ground, but none of the *Komo* membership attempted to assault the Tukulor out of the knowledge that to have done so would have brought a punitive column of Tukulor soldiery to the village to destroy it.[21]

Tauxier maintains that the *Komo* survived its confrontations with the Tukulor and that it was still intact when the French arrived in the 1890's.[22] This is an unqualified general statement that cannot be taken at face value. True the *Komo*, like other *dyow* survived, but only in some areas and in many of these it had been significantly altered by Tukulor presence. Greater integrity was maintained in areas that successfully resisted direct Tukulor military control such as the Beledougou, Sarro and the Baninko. But even in these regions, the presence of nearby powerful Moslem states exerted an intimidating influence. Other regions in the south and west came under the sporadic control of another *imam*-warrior, Samory Toure, between 1880 and 1898. But Samory's presence was not sustained, being viewed today by indigenous peoples as something akin to well-organized brigandage. Yet it did have some effect on modifying the *dyow.*

To belittle the destructive influences of these invasions on indigenous Bambara life and cults is to pander to a distorted Islamic world view and give comfort to overly sensitive modern-day Malians who would otherwise find unacceptable distress in so negative a characterization of their adopted religion. Some scholars, dependent on the good offices of Moslem officials for the succesful conduct of their field research, have gone so far as to suggest that Islam is an encouraging force for the representational arts in Africa. Such a view is not convincing, for it casts *imams* in the incongruous role of patrons of the arts.

The influence of Islam on these associations was not uniform either over time or in degree. It did not lead to a sudden functional disappearance of these groups. But in many instances it caused a disappearance of their public activities. The Moslem Tukulor ruled over most of the Bambara with an absolutist theocratic form of government and set about destroying the indigenous Bambara religion, its cults and external ritual manifestations. For this corpus of indigenous beliefs did not simply constitute a religion, but more importantly a well organized political and social force capable of challenging Tukulor hegemony.

What developed among the Bambara, in terms of the *dyow,* were changed forms, responding to the exigencies of the moment, a moment that lasted four decades. Thus what existed at the advent of the colonial period and co-incidentally with the demise of theocratic Tukulor rule represented a significant change from what had been before. The changes included the demise of some *dyow* from certain areas and modifications in the ones that survived. In place of the hierarchical structure of six *dyow,* some regions were left with only four, the *Nama, Komo* and *Kono* being telescoped into one and called by either of the three names. Favoring this development were some functional and structural commonalities shared by these *dyow.* In some areas two of these *dyow* were simply dropped

with a much altered third remaining. According to contemporary non-Moslem informants, whose information was received from antecedent generations, Tukulor antipathy was more directed against the *Komo, Kono* and *Nama* than against *Tyi Wara, N'Tomo* and *Kwore,* because of the political powers vested in the former.

Thus at the advent of colonial rule, what existed was the result of four decades of adaptive efforts on the part of an indigenous people resisting alien Moslem rule. These translated into area differences in *dyow* structure, with *Komo* present in one place, *Kono* in another, *Nama* in yet another. Still, some towns possessed all of them, but they were few in number, remembered today as faint whispers of a pre-Moslem past and of the way things used to be.

The next assault on the *dyow* came from French colonial rule. Tauxier, who was a colonial administrator, says that when Tukulor rule came to an end, the *Komo* was finished with a troublesome Moslem conquerer, but that its difficulties with the French had just begun.[23] These difficulties had their roots in two characteristics of the *Komo.* First it was a secret society, by definition dangerous, and secondly it was a powerful political and judicial group that could potentially crystalize a revolt against colonial rule. Initially the French adopted a modified tolerant attitude, going so far as to allow non-Moslem Bambara to swear by the *Komo* during judicial procedures.[24] But eventually chiefs of the *Komo* challenged the French in political matters and the latter, like the Tukulor, did not hesitate to resort to destroying the visible elements of this *dyow* and intimidating its membership. By the 1920's, the *Komo* was almost uniquely a religious association, having been divested of its political and judicial functions.[25] By definition then, it was a much altered association from what it had once been. To combat the political threat posed by the *dyow* the French actively supported the spread of Islam through direct financial subsidies for the construction of mosques and the establishment of koranic schools.

Although these actions of the colonial government had a strong negative impact on the *dyow*, they were not as significant as the effects of a newly created cash economy. Initiation was both costly and time-consuming. Dieterlen, for example, documented the demise of *Komo* branches because people viewed initiation as too costly.[26] Such a perception, however, probably occurred against a background in which belief in the *Komo* had dwindled. More importantly, young men in many villages were faced with a choice. They could spend the long months of a dry season involved with the rites and rituals of initiation societies whose relevancy was rapidly dwindling, or they could use the time to work in the cash economy, often on the coast, and thereby improve their material well being. Many opted for the latter. In addition, many young men espoused Islam, not so much out of fervent conviction but as a means of escaping from the tight social, economic and political control of the indigenous gerontocracy that ruled the Bambara.[27]

By the time of Malian independence in 1960, the *Komo* and other *dyow* were in serious decline and indeed had completely disappeared from many areas. The Malian penal code, promulgated at that time, specifically prohibits secret societies. During the two decades since independence, the government has not hesitated to vigorously move against the *dyow* as it did in 1969 when a village in the Bamako region was destroyed and its population dispersed because of *Komo* society activities in which children were sacrificed. But such dramatic confrontations are extremely rare since all of the *dyow*, wherever they still survive, have lost their political and judicial powers and are rapidly losing their relgious ones to Islam.

It is common knowledge that not all of the major six *dyow* have existed in the majority of Bambara villages in the present century. Based on this observation, McNaughton has derived a theoretical construct for explaining the absence of either the *Komo, Nama* or *Kono* from villages.[28] Essentially he attempts to refute Zahan's description of a multilayered hierarchical structure as overstated and idealized. He argues for interchangeability among the *Komo, Nama* and *Kono*. To prove this point he musters the well-known evidence that since the colonial period one of these societies has frequently existed to the exclusion of the others in specific areas. As a description of the relationship of these *dyow* to one another in the present century in many areas of Bambara land, his assessment is accurate. It runs aground, however, as a statement of *dyow* structure and relationships before the advent of the colonial period and in some areas of the Bambara country even until quite recently. McNaughton makes the cogent observation: "If the situation was different, then it must have changed some generations before the French arrived."[29] In point of fact that is precisely what happened under the Tukulor.

It is of interest that during the period of *dyow* attrition, individuals often traveled to distant villages to be initiated into societies absent in their own villages. Like obtaining graduate degrees, they traveled to where the best knowledge was being offered and took great pride in having been initiated in villages respected for the quality of specific *dyow*. Those who were initiated into all of the six major *dyow* were held in very high esteem by family and neighbors. This tradition of studying at a distance from one's native village has been continued by Moslem Bambara. Those who aspire to become Moslem clerics (*marabout*) not only study under local clerics who enjoy regional esteem, but also go to centers like Djenne and even Timbuctoo to both acquire knowledge and to establish personal legitimacy and esteem as men of great holiness and power.

Chapter 2

A General Overview of the *Dyo* and *Gouan* Societies

Contextual information about the sculptures associated with the six major *dyow* has been provided by a number of scholars. The same cannot be said, however, for the ritual objects once used by the southern Bambara and Bambarized Senufo in two *dyow*, the *Dyo* and the *Gouan* (*Guan, Gwan*). These associations once flourished in the "land around the rivers," a vast expanse of wooded savanna country, flood plains and swamps drained by three affluents of the Bani River, the Baule, Bagoe and Banifing (Ngorolaka). This area extends from the eastern part of the Bougouni cercle, through parts of the Dioila and Sikasso cercles to the western borders of the Koutiala cercle.

Pinpointing the geographic distribution of these associations, as well as other Bambara ones, by using modern administrative units is less than satisfactory because such units are often subject to changes in size and name. Indeed, Mali's 1977 administrative reform created new cercles, renamed existing ones and shifted cercle borders. The use of indigenous names for areas is more satisfactory, but it must be remembered that these two are vulnerable to change, less dramatic and frequent to be sure, but brought about by the intrusion of newer outside ethnic elements.

The northernmost distribution of the *Dyo* was in the Baninko (land beyond the Bani), an area that lies around the confluence of the Baule and Bagoe Rivers and the initial course of the Bani River which arises from them. However, the *Dyo* was principally found further south, in the Banimounitie, a region north of the town of Bougouni and northeast and east of Bougouni in Massigui and Kinian. The latter area is about sixty miles north of the town of Sikasso. In the area of its northern distribution, villages with the *Dyo* interfaced with those possessing the *Kwore*. The *Gouan* had a less extensive distribution than the *Dyo*, being limited to the southern tier of the Baninko and areas around and to the east of Bougouni.

The *Dyo* and the *Gouan* were affected by all of the forces already discussed. In addition, the decline of these societies was aided by the spread of river blindness (onchocerciasis). This fly transmitted disease became endemic in the southern Bambara country, resulting in permanent blindness in many adults. This led to serious economic and social consequences and to an exodus of people from the area. To deal with river blindness, the French colonial administration employed mobile medical teams and moved populations away from river and stream beds that are the fly's preferred habitat. This measure was mistakenly interpreted by the local population as an attempt on the part of the French to move them closer to administrative centers for the purpose of taxation. It is true that the French moved people closer to administrative centers, but only because these centers were purposely built in areas considered disease free.

Another major influence on the *Dyo* and *Gouan* was the large scale recruitment of men for the armed forces by the French during both world wars. This recruitment effort not only removed large numbers of critical members for long periods of time, but also intensively exposed these recruits to the outside western world. Because the Bambara of the Bougouni region enjoyed a reputation as good riflemen, recruitment was especially intense among them. In the 1960's and 1970's there was hardly an area in the southern Bambara country that did not have *anciens combattants*. Wherever I met them, they would often give their matriculation number, remembered over a half century in the case of

World War I veterans and recite the battles in which they had participated. Balesi has written a detailed account of these World War I veterans from French West Africa.[1]

The *Dyo* can be viewed as a southern variant of the *Kwore* society, an association that was once present in much of the eastern, central and northern Bambara country. The two organizations shared similar internal structures, external ritual manifestations, goals and overall functions. And both were simultaneously regligious cults and cultural organizations. Yet there were differences between them and significantly in how they related to the *Komo*. While the *Kwore* complemented the *Komo,* the *Dyo* excluded it and vice versa. This paradox had its roots in the fact that the *Dyo* essentially encompassed the religious, social and judicial content of not only the *Komo* and *Kwore* but also the *Nama* and *Tyi Wara*.[2] Zahan cogently speculates that the *Dyo* may in fact have been the primordial society out of whose groups the principal Bambara *dyow* emerged through a process of progressive expansion.[3]

It is important to remember that the *Dyo* and *Gouan* also existed among Bambara and Bambarized Senufo whose status was peripheral both culturally and geographically to the center of the Bambara world at Segou.

The first written mention of the *Dyo* was provided by Henry who summarily described it as a fetish.[4] Tauxier provided some additional functional details in characterizing it as an ancient fetish on which sworn statements were made. He wrote: ". . . One digs a hole and places in it a knife, a hatchet, a hoe, some keys, arrows and even rifle shot. One adds on top a large stone and even tree roots, then one carefully closes it. It is on this that one oaths and if one perjures oneself, the divinity kills you."[5] In 1953, Viviana Paques undertook an extensive study of the *Dyo* in the Bougouni Cercle.[6] This writer made his observations between 1967 and 1974, in the cercles of Bougouni, Dioila, Koutiala, Kolokani, Bla and Sikasso. By this time, much of what Paques had described two decades before had become historical.

Interestingly, the first time that *Gouan* statuary was accurately identified in print by its Bambara name was on a 1973 Air Mail calendar. A large modern seated female figure sculpted in wood and holding an infant was correctly captioned "Gouandousou."

The first substantial information on the *Gouan* was published in 1974.[7] It was described as a fertility cult present in the Baninko region of the southern Bambara country. Additionally, detailed information was provided about Gouandousou, large wooden statues of seated women holding babies. These statutes and those of standing men and women and men on horseback were central to the cult. The Gouandousou and other wooden female statues of the *Gouan* cult have been frequently called "queens" and indeed "Bambara Queens," in catalogue descriptions prepared by a number of writers. From certain perspectives, this is not an entirely inaccurate characterization. However, it has not been derived form any first hand knowledge of contextual use but from statuary architectonics suggestive of regality.

In 1981, Ezra, provided some stylistic and thematic analyses of *Gouan* statuary in an exhibition catalogue of the Metropolitan Museum of Art. In addition, she furnished some brief descriptions of the *Gouan* society, based on field observations made in 1978.[8]

The Relationship Between The *Dyo* and The *Gouan*

There were essentially two distinct types of relationships between the *Dyo* and the *Gouan* in recent years. In some villages the *Gouan* was perceived as an integral part of the *Dyo*, a relationship that was also documented by Ezra in 1978.[9] In other villages it was considered a distinct society, entry into which was contingent on seven years of previous membership in the *N'Tokofa* group of the *Dyo*. Members of other *Dyo* groups in these areas were not eligible for *Gouan* membership. This resulted in a high ratio of *Dyo* to *Gouan* and a positive correlation between *N'Tokofa* and *Gouan*.

Part of the difficulty in determining whether or not the *Gouan* was a distinct society from the *Dyo* lies in the fact that the

Dyo itself was composed of several distinct groups. The religious, social, political, judicial and ritual content of these groups was sufficiently distinct to give them the appearance of separate societies. Yet they were coordinated at varing levels and integrated in the sacerdotal body that directed them.

While some villages possessed all *Dyo* groups, more often than not, villages possessed only one or two groups. And an even smaller number of villages possessed the *Gouan*. The fact that *Gouan* initiation was contingent for many on previous membership in the *Dyo* does not necessarily make a strong case for the former being an integral part of the latter. *Kwore* initiation for example, was contingent on previous *N'Tomo* initiation which was also required for induction into the *Komo*. Yet the three were distinct societies. Even identical leadership of the *Dyo* and the *Gouan* does not necessarily imply that they were part of one association. The same indivduals, for example, simultaneously headed more than one *dyow*. What is more germaine to this debate, is how the relationship between the *Dyo* and the *Gouan* was perceived by those who were members. This writer found during extensive field investigations that the *Gouan* was simultaneously perceived as being distinct from the *Dyo* by some and as an integral part of it by others. The former view was frequently held by people from areas where *Gouan* initiation was restricted to the *N'Tokofa* membership. This view might have been expected because large numbers of people were excluded from entry into the *Gouan*.

Interestingly, the *Gouan* cult was transported several hundred miles to a village in the Kolokani cercle in the early 1940's by men who were *Kwore* initiates and who were working in the Dioila cercle with the Public Works Department. It functioned in this village for about two decades albeit in a much modified form. In this village *Gouan* membership bore a direct relationship to previous *Kwore* initiation.

Dyo Groups

Paques relates that the *Dyo* consisted of four societies: *N'Kenie, N'Tokofa, Dyoburu* and *Basso*.[10] Blacksmiths, however, were not members of any of these groups, having one of their own, *Duga*.[11] Interestingly, villages that had the *N'Kenie* and the *N'Tokofa* did not have blacksmiths. Thus whatever representational art forms they used were made elsewhere. In some areas, however, many informants related to this writer that the *Dyo* encompassed seven groups. These were: *N'Kenie, N'Tokofa, Dyomburu, M'Para Sien, Soma, Duga* and *Gouan*. Of these seven, four are identical to those described by Paques. She correctly related that little was known at the time of her study of the social organization of the peoples who practiced the *Dyo* and this coupled to the secret nature of *Dyo* groups impeded a fuller understanding of the *Dyo* itself. Thus, she wrote, "We are far from arriving at a total comprehension of these institutions."[12] Despite this disclaimer, a great debt of thanks is owed to Paques for her superb detailed descriptions of the *Dyo* groups she studied and for providing excellent details on the metaphysical and cosmological ideas that were the foundation upon which these groups stood.

Chapter 3
The Myths of Creation

A large corpus of complex mythological and metaphysical beliefs underlie both the *Dyo* and *Gouan* societies. For the most part, this corpus constitutes esoteric knowledge known only to a small group of elderly men and women. Part of it consists of the myth of creation, of which there are numerous versions in the Bambara country. Scholars such as de Ganay, Dieterlen, Paques and Zahan have provided detailed descriptions of the myth of creation as they recorded it in various regions inhabited by the Bambara. In 1963, Zahan published a succinct overview of the creation myth as documented by all of these researchers.[1] The Bambara creation myth and all of the events which emanate from it represent ideal constructs. They define the world and the conduct of human affairs according to ideal norms that are rarely found in reality. Whether these norms actually existed in the real world during previous historical periods is a matter of debate. We will simply never know for sure. But based on my many years of research among the Bambara, I am inclined to think that they were only rarely found in reality. This does not lessen their importance, however, because they constitute desired standards towards which a number of non-Moslem Bambara still strive.

Bambara metaphysical thought and mythology can be found in Bambara iconography. Yet only those who possess deep and esoteric knowledge can see these messages that are embodied in the architectonics of a statue for example or in the surface designs of a mask. For other people, ordinary people, the messages sent out by these sculptures are quite different. These messages are understandably linked to people's level of knowledge, to their knowledge of the real world and the supernatural world they have been told about.

The *Gouan* society is an especially good example for demonstrating that cultural phenomena often fit into several frameworks and not merely into one. It dramatically shows that even in the area of esoteric conceptual constructs there are regional variations, in this case because there are regional versions of the creation myth that substantially differ from one another. In addition, there are perceptions of the *Gouan* by initiates lacking deep knowledge and perceptions of non-initiated witnesses. These perceptions and interpretations are almost invariably linked to larger cultural phenomena. Thus for example, some of the southern Bambara see the *Gouan* as an ancestor cult. This is not surprising because ancestor cults devoted to specific village founders are extremely common among them. Yet those Bambara to the north of them, in the Baninko, who lack deep knowledge, do not see the *Gouan* as a cult primarily devoted to a specific ancestor but rather to ancestral women in general, to a collectivity of ancestral women spirits.

Thus there is no easy answer to the often posed question about the symbolism of the large seated female statues that were central to the society. These statues as well as all of the sculptures and material elements of the society held different meanings for different people. And it is reasonable to assume that these meanings were never static from one generation to the next. To claim that explanations of symbolism based on mythology are more valid than the common man's view is just as erroneous as to argue that they are less relevant because they are only known to a small group of people. All Bambara interpretations have validity and for this reason and to better understand both the *Dyo* and *Gouan* societies, it is worth looking at them in some depth.

The myth of creation known to the southern Bambara is essentially that described by Paques.[2] Compared to the myth found further to the north, from which it differs considerably, it is strikingly depersonalized.

While the myth around Segou, the Baninko and even in certain areas of Bougouni contains supernatural personalities embodying known human virtues and weaknesses, the southern myth revolves around non-human beings and forces. Thus it is not surprising, as will be described later, that some of the southern Bambara with esoteric knowledge, interpret the *Gouan* as a cult devoted to a specific historical ancestor of the post-creation period. Yet they see in the *Dyo* and its material expressions many of the depersonalized elements of the myth of creation as they know it. This is also not surprising because the *Dyo* readily lends itself to this kind of interpretive treatment whereas the *Gouan* does not. These interpretations of the *Dyo* were not widely known in the north where there is some interdigitation with the *Kwore* society.

What is presented here is basically a summary of the myth of creation as outlined by Paques in her treatise on the *Dyo*.[3] I have emphasized only those points that have particular relevance to the material expressions of the society. The southern Bambara believe in a supreme being who created man in the image of his finger. God is heat, stillness and silence. True creation, known as *manazo*, emanated from God. He created all things through his vibrating spirit known as *yo*, and through his index finger. His first creation was fire that is light, heat, sound, movement and a generating power. This fire formed *segi lolo*, the buffalo star, that is also the star of circumcision. *Segi lolo* existed long before any other creation and contained all future creation. Eventually the earth appeared as a humid principle. The intelligible sky, symbolized by *segi lolo*, and the earth were connected to one another by the *banagolo* tree that had seventeen branches. This tree is symbolized on earth today by the *bana* tree *(Ceiba pentandra)*. It is a ladder over which the *ni* component of the human soul ascends to heaven at the time of death. The *dya* or double resides in the family altar. The *ni* may come down from heaven and enter the womb of a pregnant female member of the family. Sacrifices are made to ancestors in order to nourish them and they in turn reward their

kin on earth with fertility and rain. The seventeen equal branches of the *bana* tree represent eight twin ancestor couples plus God at the top. The couple at the bottom represents the earth, and the seven others the heavens. On the left side of the tree there are six ancestors, three males and three females. On the right, there are eight, four males and four females. God and the earth are connected by a continuous line formed by this succession of men and women. A stair like line within this vertical structure symbolizes the python moving ahead in expanding life. Turning over on itself, the python symbolizes a transformation of life. This step like line connecting vertical levels of ancestors finds expression in woven cloth depicting three parallel lines of alternating black and white squares. These three lines symbolize the triple python that represents a continuous route of blood and fertility.

All creation is composed of four parts except the python which has but two, a head symbolizing God and a body. The mythical python, symbolized by earthly ones, was created by the rays of the sun falling on the earth. The python is viewed as being in perpetual movement between the humid earth and the sky.

The *bana* tree connects to seven heavens that eventually lead to God whose direction is indicated by the rainbow. The first heaven is that of scorpions and twins. Both are symbolically associated with rain and fertility. The seventh heaven is that of the white cock. His sounds, which are fertility blessings, descend through the other heavens to earth, picking up their powers enroute. The southern Bambara view the white cock as the best animal for making sacrifices to ancestors.

The first fire eventually entered a stone. It also gave a portion of itself to every living thing, but stones remained its principal receptacle. While the fire in every living thing eventually lessens and death ensues, that in stone does not. Thus stone is the perpetual abode of the first fire. The stone in which the first fire resided found itself in the middle of a lake. Four first signs came forth from the fire, setting up the cardinal points of the earth. From these developed *Bemba*, viewed as the first human ancestor. As will be seen further on, *Bemba* is regarded by other Bambara as God. All created things had four parts, head, neck, stomach and legs. *Bemba* is the image of the stone, which is fire, derived from God's fingernail. He went to the east and from him came a second sign in the form of a trident. It was the neck and it went to the north and is considered the earth, derived from the second finger of God. A third sign emanated from the others and went to the west. It is the element water and the stomach or heart. It derived from the third finger of God's hand. From it came a double sign in the form of a bird's beak, constituting the legs and air. It was these four principal signs that then created man near the lake. Thus he is composed of four signs, fire, earth, water and air, and seven parts, head, stomach, vertebral column, two arms and two legs.

This version of the myth of creation expresses itself in the southern and western Bambara country in tangible form in sacred ponds and lakes that contain prominent stones that are the focus of veneration. Fire and water are also often represented by two mountains in this region, between which the mythical python is believed to move. In so doing he promotes progressive creation, and maintains contact between the earth and the sky. Within the *Dyo* society, elements of this mythology are symbolized in stones which are viewed as the abode of the first fire and in the triple serpent motif found on the costumes of some Dyo members and depicted in irons of the *Gouan* society. *Dyo* society members wear a cock's comb headdress or one sculpted in the form of a rainbow, essential elements in the creation myth. The frequent presence of seven drums or seven horns in *Dyo* groups is viewed by Paques as a reflection of the creation process in seven elements as is the time period between initiation cycles, namely seven years. The musical instruments of a *Dyo* group are often said to be offspring of a mother instrument, a point made by Paques and one confirmed by myself. This mother instrument is believed to be integrated into the essence of *segi lolo*, the buffalo star and the original creative fire of the world.

A much more personalized creation myth is found in the northern area of *Dyo* and *Gouan* distribution. It is quite akin to the myth known to the Segou Bambara. Zahan has provided an excellent summary of this myth whose essential elements are presented here.[4] I have added to it relevant points about the *Dyo* and *Gouan*.

The Bambara believe in a supreme being known by a number of names such as *N'gala* and *Bemba*. Closely associated with him and with the act of creation are several supernatural beings. Prominent among them are *Mousso Koroni Koundye* or *Nyale, Faro* and *Ndomadyiri*. From a certain perspective these beings are also a manifestation of God. During the first phase of creation, known as *dali folo*, the earth was naked and God manifested himself as a grain (*kise*) known as *Pemba*. A *balanza* tree (*Acacia albida*) grew from this seed. But when it became fully grown, it withered and fell to the ground. Eventually, all that remained was a long beam of wood, known as *Pembele*. This wood beam secreted mildew that accumulated beneath it. *Pembele* mixed this mildew with his own saliva to create a new being, a female, known as *Mousso Koroni Koundye* (little old woman with white head). It is this being who is central to the *Gouan* cult for some of the Bambara.

Mousso Koroni then engaged in the creative process, engendering vegetables, animals and human beings. The latter were then immortal. Her creativity was characterized by disorder, confusion and haste. This is excused by some Bambara on the grounds that she wanted to people the earth with beings as rapidly as possible. Finally *Mousso Koroni* planted the *Pembele* in the ground and he became a tree once again. Men worshipped *Pemba*, now a *balanza* tree, the tree that eventually introduced them to death. In time, men transferred their worship to *Faro*, another supernatural being and manifestation of God, who is the master of water.

As Zahan points out, some Bambara believe that *Mousso Koroni* disappeared at this point, after spending a wretched life on earth authoring disorder. Others, however, including *Dyo* and *Gouan* initiates, believe that she continues to live, the personification of air, wind and fire. She is also the "mother of magic," the first sorcerer and as such is called by another name, *Nyale.*

Mousso Koroni was originally created with a soul that had two parts, like those of all human beings. But at the time of her creation, while God gave her the *ni,* he entrusted its double, the *dya* to *Faro.* Thus *Mousso Koroni* was incomplete from the moment of her creation. Nonetheless, she authored the first phrase of creation, characterized by prodigious growth and fertility. As Zahan says, as *Nyale,* she gives strength to newborns and hastens the ripening of grain. She is the source of all human ideas, which have been or will be given to man and represents energy, activity and desire. But she is also the source of all malice, misunderstanding, treachery and sorcery. She is an extravagant being, unruly, uncontrolled and excessive. She causes everything to proliferate, but in an uncontrolled manner.

In entrusting *Mousso Koroni*'s dya to *Faro,* God in effect set limits on the amount of disorder in the world. He also deprived the primordial female being of coherence and made her defective. It could be cogently argued that the ancient Bambara conceived of this component of the myth to rationalize woman's inferior position in their society and the necessity for male dominance.

The second phase of creation, called *dali flani,* was dominated by *Faro* and *Ndomadyiri.* The former represents equilibrium and the latter stability. *Faro* is believed to be androgynous and to live in water. But in drawings and in sculpture, he is represented in female form with long hair, breasts and a fish tail. Moslem Bambara view him today as a water genie. *Faro* is associated with thunder and lightning, rain and rainbows. His role is to perfect the world, orgainize it, put it in equilibrium and give it eternal life. As Zahan explains, *Faro* was born of God's vaporous breath, from a bubble of his saliva while God was pronouncing the words of creation. *Faro* is also the visible countenance of God, a countenance that is white. *Faro* is in a sense God's word, but during this second phase of creation, this word was unintelligible to humans, consisting of a language in which all words were connected.

It was *Ndomadyiri,* the divine blacksmith, the third supernatural person after *Mousso Koroni* and *Faro,* who made this primordial word into useful language. He is, as Zahan says, what is left, the earth, after the evaporation of water (*Faro*) due to the action of the wind (*Nyale*). This provokes the notion of fixity, of remaining in place after the withdrawal of his previous associations. So the Bambara see him symbolized in trees, fixed and powerful living beings, the source of the first life, *Mousso Koroni.* Some see him as a tree and thus as master of herbs and remedies and a healer, a characteristic of all blacksmiths. Thus *Ndomadyiri* is the eponymous ancestor of all blacksmiths, and the author of all healing. *Faro* and *Ndomadyiri* complement one another. *Faro* represents water and rain, needed for life while *Ndomadyiri* is the earth and has stability and provides man with a home.

The third phase of creation is that of the present. As Zahan observes, it is the stage when human beings and things confront one another. The formation of human societies results in confusion and disorder due to men assserting themselves and expressing their wills and emotions. *Ndomadyiri,* however, as a blacksmith, is omnipresent, stabilizing society through his supervision of its religious rites.

Mousso Koroni, who had retreated during the second phase of creation appeared again during the third as *Nyale.* While the second phase was characterized by order, balanace and harmony, the third has great potential for the disorder and confusion characteristic of the first phase. Again, a male dominated society which relegates women to an inferior political and social position, produces powerful religious and metaphysical reasons for so doing.

Known in this last ongoing phase as *Nyale, Mousso Koroni* represents activity, energy, mystery, desire, secrecy and as Zahan so well explains, taste for all that man wants to achieve. She is unbounded enthusiasm, and extravagance, but also a source of fertility and creation. If left to the influences of *Nyale* alone, man would indulge in all manner of excesses and society would break down. That is why *Ndomadyiri* is present, to control and set limits.

As Zahan cogently reasons, the Bambara myth of creation contains both good and bad elements. *Mousso Koroni* cannot totally disappear because she is the source of all activity, animation, rivalry and very importantly, courage. The world cannot progress without her. But left alone, her influence would result in a complete breakdown of creation. Thus *Ndomadyiri* is needed as a counterweight of stability. In a sense, as Zahan says, *Nyale* and *Ndomadyiri* are diametrically opposed principles. It is *Faro* who provides a balance between the two.

Mousso Koroni was *Pemba's* wife during the first phase of creation when she created all animal and vegetable life. It was he who suggested that she cultivate wild cereals in order to better their quality. She knew that the spitting cobra (*Naja nigricollis*), *n'gorogo* in Bambara, could help her in this task. She coupled with him and gave birth to a creature, called *Tyi Wara*. This being began farming with the claws of his feet, a metal weapon given to him by his mother and his hooded snake's head, shaped like a hoe. He fertilized the soil with his venom, taught men the techniques for farming and gave them the courage to carry them out.[5] As will be discussed later, *Mousso Koroni's* relationship with the snake is seen symbolically by some Bambara in some of the iron staffs once used by the *Gouan* society.

The most dramatic sculptures of the society, however, are large wooden statues of women which, at a profound level of knowledge, represent *Nyale* (*Mousso Koroni*) and wooden statues of men that represent *Ndomadyiri*. Together, these statues symbolize balanced and ordered creation. It is most noteworthy that leadership roles in the *Gouan* were assigned to either women born out of wedlock or to women without brothers. Both represent undesirable social situations and departures from the norm. They symbolize the handiwork of *Nyale* in the world today and of *Mousso Koroni* in the first phase of creation. As such they are *Nyale's* ideal representatives.

1. *Village in the southern Bambara country, December, 1974.*

2. _Tyi Wara_ society dancers, Boussin, April, 1970.

4. *N'Tomo dancer being accompanied to the village square by age set association members, Senou, March, 1971.*

3. *N'Tomo dancer, Sirakoro, April, 1971.*

5. *Gouandousou statue of the "northern style," depicted with a talisman covered bamada hat and a chain of diamond shaped forms representing the creative powers of the serpent. Wood, Height, 48.6 inches.*

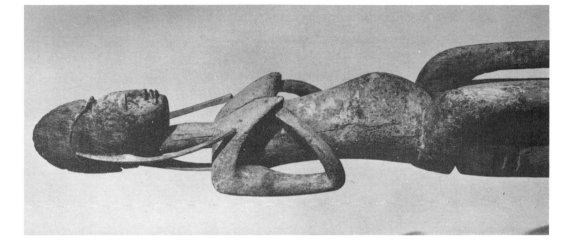

6. _Gouantigui statue depicted with a
bamada hat and an inverted horn
holding medicines. Some Bambara
believe that these statues represent
Ndomadyiri, the heavenly blacksmith
who is also the master of herbal
medicines. Wood, Height, 42.7 inches._

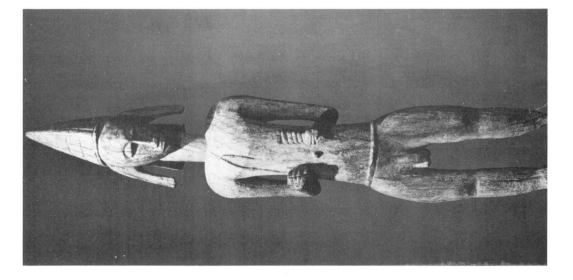

7. _Gouandousou statue of the "northern
style," depicted with a rainbow shaped
head crest and a pregnant abdomen.
Some Bambara believe that these statues represent an historical ancestor, or
else the collectivity of female ancestors. Others believe they symbolize
Mousso Koroni (Nyale), a female
supernatural being who authored
much of creation. Wood, Height, 44.5 inches._

8. *N'Tokofa* members, Sola, 1953.

9. *N'Kenie* orchestra, Sola, 1953.

11. *The* _buruba_ *(mother trumpet) of the Dyoburu, Gualamina, 1953.*

10. _N'Kenie_ *initiate with an n'keniamba, the mother drum symbolizing* _segi lolo_, *the circumcision star, Sola, 1953.*

12. *The two principal twin trumpets of the* <u>*Dyoburu,*</u> *Gualamina, 1953.*

13. *The smallest trumpet of the* <u>*Dyoburu,*</u> *Gualamina, 1953.*

14. *Blacksmiths of the* <u>*N'Keribadjo*</u> *performing on a village square. The three small wooden statues in the foreground are* <u>*Dyonyeni*</u> *sculpted with the rainbow head crest that symbolizes the direction of God, Youroubadougou, 1953.*

15. *Blacksmiths of the* <u>*N'Keribadjo*</u>, *Youroubadougou, 1953.*

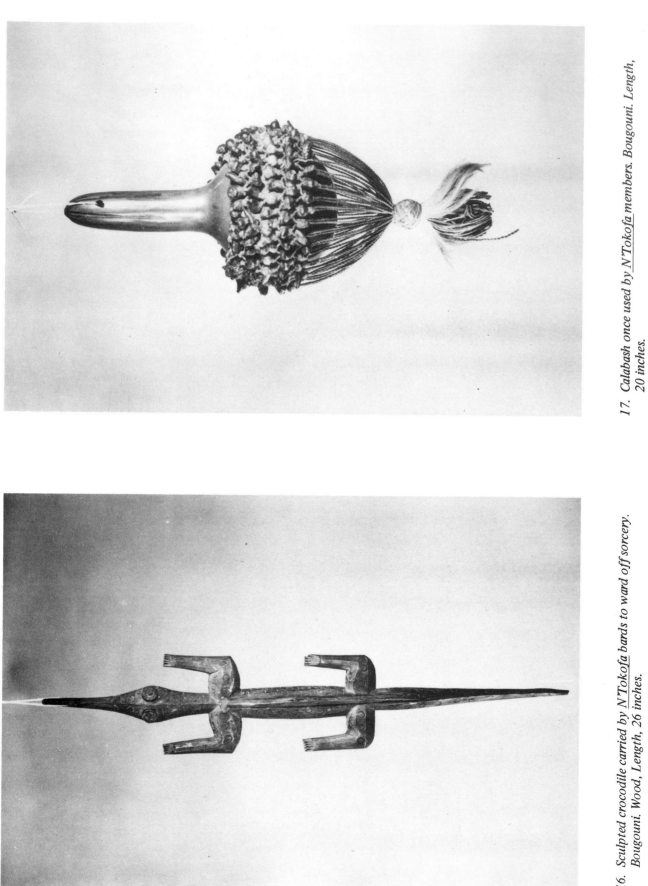

17. *Calabash once used by N'Tokofa members. Bougouni. Length, 20 inches.*

16. *Sculpted crocodile carried by N'Tokofa bards to ward off sorcery. Bougouni. Wood, Length, 26 inches.*

18. _Gouan_ society irons depicting _Gouantigui._ Dioila. Height, 7 inches.

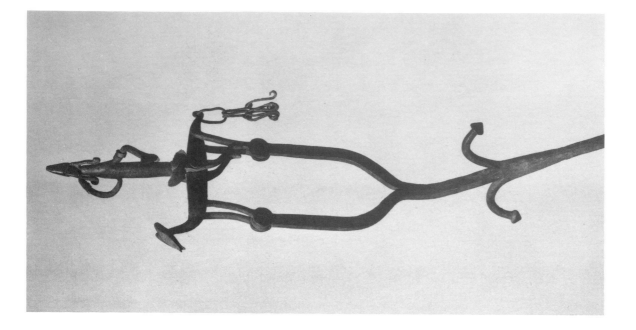

20. *Gouan society staff depicting Gouantigui on the back of an animal whose head is stylized into that of a serpent's. Dioila. Iron, Height, 24 inches.*

19. *Gouan society staff depicting Gouandousou, symbolizing Mousso Koroni (Nyale), and a trident of serpents, representing the triple python, symbol of progressive and continuous creation. Dioila. Iron, Height, 24.7 inches.*

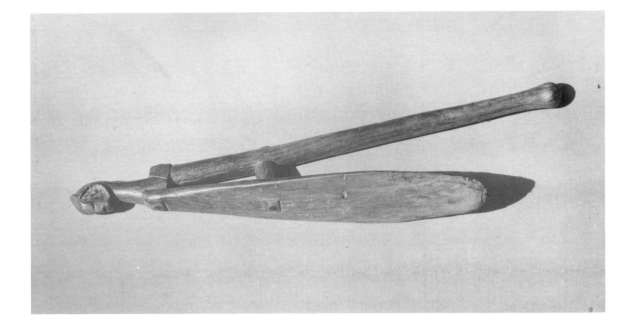

22. *Ceremonial hoe of the Tyi Wara society depicting a human head and the hood of the cobra, Segou. Wood, Height, 30 inches.*

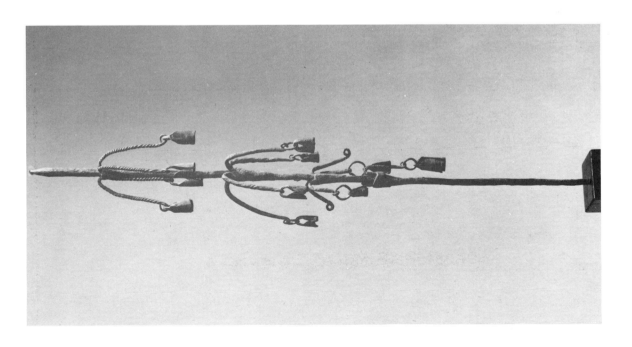

21. *Dyo society staff representing the serpent, symbol of light, progressive creation and time. Bougouni. Iron, Height, 30 inches.*

24. *Head of* tium *drum of the* N'Kenie *society shown in Figure 23.*

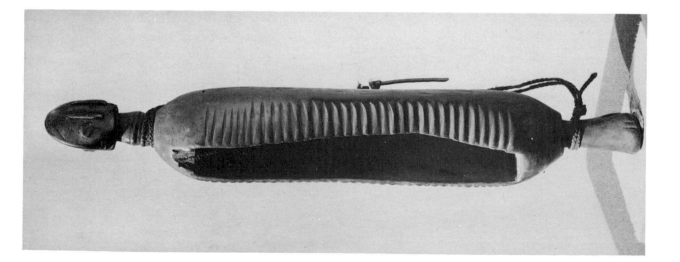

23. N'Kenie *drum of the* tium *type. Dioila.* Wood, Height, 36 inches.

26. *Buruba (mother trumpet) of the Dyoburu society.* *The two finger-like forms on the head represent the open mouth of the crocodile, a powerful anti-sorcery symbol. Dioila. Wood, Height, 40 inches.*

25. *N'Kenie drum of the tierum type.* Dioila. Wood, Height, 28 inches.

27. _Gouan_ statue that could be of either the _Gouandousou or Gouan Nyeni_
    variety. Wood, Height, 44.4 inches.

29. *Closeup of Figure 28 showing the soft rounded facial features and details of the bamada hat. The open mouth of the crocodile is well depicted in the folds of the hat as is the crocodile's tail in the hat's flap. Both are powerful anti-sorcery symbols.*

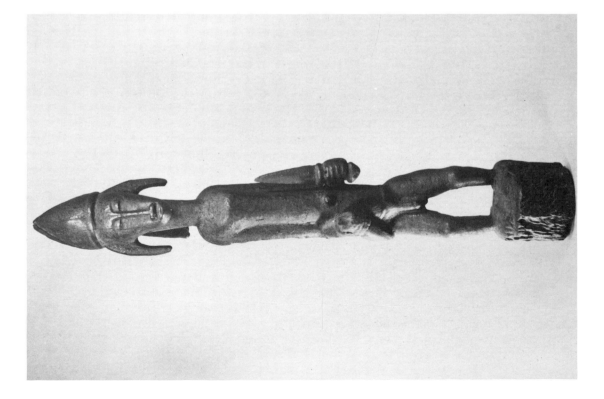

28. *Gouantigui statue with the bamada hat and an upturned sword. It and the Gouandousou statue depicted on the cover constitute a pair and were housed in the same village shrine. Dioila. Wood, Height, 36 inches.*

31. *Gouan Nyeni statue of the "northern style" depicted with two side hair tresses. This statue bears none of the power symbols usually shown on* Gouandousou *statues. Bougouni. Wood, Height, 45 inches.*

30. *Gouantigui depicted as a horseman holding up a sword. Although this figure retains many of the architectonics peculiar to Gouan statuary, the facial features and conical Moslem hat indicate it was sculpted at a more recent date. Bougouni. Wood, Height, 33 inches.*

32. _Dyonyeni statue of an N'Tokofa group. The lower torso is encircled by a plaited mass of vegetable fibers impregnated with mud, representing the costuming of N'Tokofa buffoons. Dioila. Wood. Height, 21 inches. Exhibited at "Manding: Focus On An African Civilisation," The British Museum, 1972._

33. _Dyonyeni statue of an N'Kenie group. Dioila. Wood, Height, 21 inches._

35. Large wooden statue that may or may not have been used by the Gouan society. Wood, Height, 46.8 inches.

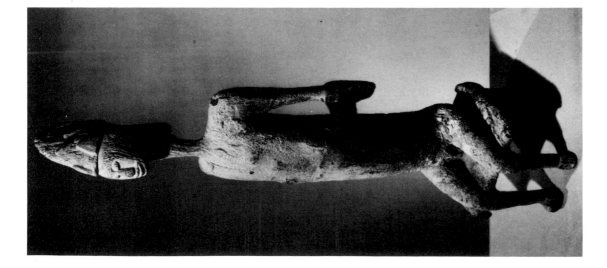

34. Seated figure of <u>Gouantigui</u> shown wearing a talisman covered bamada hat. Statues showing this posture are rare. Wood, Height, 38.5 inches.

Chapter 4

Rituals and Functions

The rituals of both the *Dyo* and *Gouan* were intertwined to some degree in many villages. They were frequently held simultaneously. Consequently they must be discussed together in order to convey a clear idea of what transpired at specific periods of the year and on given occasions.

Sanctuaries

As Paques has explained, the *Dyo* encompassed not only a corpus of metaphysical beliefs but sanctuaries, a clergy, a membership, funeral rites for members and public ceremonies.[1] The same held true for the *Gouan*. But it must be remembered that the *Gouan* frequently possessed an identical clergy and male memberships to which were added women who had not undergone *Dyo* initiation. Paques reports that all ritual objects of the *Dyo* were kept in a single village sanctuary, which also housed the objects belonging to other cults.[2] On the basis of my own field research, I can confirm this and add that *Gouan* objects were also housed in this sanctuary. These sanctuaries were usually just outside villages in wooded plots. Paques found that they were situated in woods composed of *Combretum micrantum* trees.[3] However, there were departures from this rule. Each sanctuary contained a stone submerged in water and a metal spear known as *n'tama*, a wooden sword and a hoe.[4] In addition, several fetishes were kept in a sanctuary. These were the *niaga*, a bundle of wood and roots about five feet tall, covered with white cotton and the *wara* consisting of three sacs.[5] These were all viewed as protectors of a village. The sculpted objects of village *Dyo* groups were also kept in the sanctuary, including musical instruments and statues. And as mentioned above, the *Gouan* statues were housed in these structures as well. It is important to note that the *n'keniamba,* a large

canoe shaped drum with striated sides, was considered the most important musical instrument in the sanctuary since it was viewed as the mother of all the other instruments.[6]

Clergy

The chief of a local *Dyo* chapter was known as the *Dyo Sia.* This position was often not actively sought, except by very old men because its holders were required to remain chaste, even if married, stay within the village during the rainy season and have their food prepared and clothes washed by men. The restrictions imposed on the holders of this office were sufficient for some newly elected ones to flee an area.[7] Election was often restricted to certain patronymic groups who usually had achieved a dominant political status in antecedant periods. Control of the *Dyo* was an added means of exerting social and political control. In general, *Dyo* leaders were the oldest initiates alive and often of sufficiently advanced age as to not be incovenienced by the taboos of the office. In some villages, once the choice had been made and ratified through oracular consultation with the *n'keniamba*, the candidate had a magical bonnet thrust on his head from behind.[8]

Dyo Sia Burial Vaults

The Bougouni region of Mali is well known among the *cognoscenti* for its underground burial vaults. Some of these house the remains of *Dyo Sia* and those of their wives who were simultaneously interred with them. However, not all such vaults were for *Dyo Sia* as other individuals were interred in them as well. From the structural appearance of some of these vaults, they were probably ancient iron mines subsequenly used for burials. The vaults in the Bougouni region were first discovered by Mousnier-Lompre in 1912 and commented on by Delafosse in 1913.[9] Paques explored the tomb of a *Dyo Sia* in 1953 in the Banimounitie area and provided a detailed description of its contents.[10] It should be pointed out that the underground burial vaults in the southern Bambara country bear many similarities to some I explored in the Dogon country in 1970.

What is pertinent about the contents of *Dyo Sia* burial vaults to the present discussion is the fact that some are considered female and some male. Paques' informants told her that the feminine objects present in the vault she explored were substitutes for the wives who should have been interred with the *Dyo Sia*. Such substitution began during the Moslem rule of Samory Toure whose chiefs prohibited the practice of burying wives of *Dyo Sia* at the time of the latter's death. Paques, however, correctly wondered if the grave gifts symbolized the perceived feminine nature of the *Dyo Sia* and whether a male complement existed in another village.[11]

During my field research, I was able to confirm Paques' supposition that both *Dyo Sia* and *Dyo* chapters were considered either male or female. Of great importance is the fact that *Gouandousou* statues were found in the sanctuaries of female *Dyo* chapters. Their complementary statues, *Gouantigui*, standing males, seated males or males on horseback were kept in the sanctuaries of male *Dyo* chapters. Eventually, the male-female distinction between *Dyo* chapters and leaders broke down as did the rules governing where the statues were kept. Eventually in some villages both *Gouandousou* and *Gouantigui* statues came to be housed in the same sanctuary.

This male-female differentiation is also seen in the ritual irons once kept in *Dyo* shrines and in some of the *n'tama* (spears) used by the society. It ultimately refers to the necessary balance between *Nyale* and *Ndomadyiri* for the harmonious progress of the creative process.

Initiation

All the circumcised males except those of some patronymic groups were eligible for *Dyo* initiation, and indeed all had to be initated. As Paques mentions, a family with no sons was required to have one of their unmarried excised daughters initiated.[12] Another group of women who were eligible for membership were the unmarried excised daughters of unmarried women.[13] These two groups of women had leadership roles in the *Gouan* into which they were later initiated, provided their *Dyo* chapters were affiliated with the former. Initiation into the *Dyo* usually took place every seven years. Those men and the two groups just mentioned were then eligible for *Gouan* initiation. Women who were not *Dyo* initiates, and who belonged to the next youngest age set as them were eligible at this time for *Gouan* initiation. Thus the female membership of the *Gouan* consisted of two categories of women, those with previous *Dyo* membership and those without it.

Initiation into the *Dyo* began in late April or early May, near the beginning of the rainy season which is earlier in this part of Mali than it is further north near Bamako. Initiation into the *Gouan* took place at the same time, some initiates having already spent seven years in a group of the *Dyo*. *Dyo* initiates were referred to as *kiba* and spent anywhere from a few weeks to several months in initiation rituals directed by the *Dyo Sia*. During this time they were isolated in the bush in a camp near the shrine that housed *Dyo* ritual objects. Paques has described *Dyo* initiation in some detail.[14] The first phase of initiation terminated with a ritual lighting of the bush fire that generally precedes tilling. Such fire lighting was also characteristic of the *Komo* and there was much regional variation both in the *Komo* and the *Dyo* as to how it was done. As Paques has splendidly described, the fire represents the first Bambara ancestor, real fire that came from the principal fire.[15] In engaging in these fire rituals, the Bambara gave religious meaning and symbolism to an act crucial to the survival of a slash and burn agricultural society. It is noteworthy that similar rituals are still carried out, but associated with circumcision and excision ceremonies. In the Kinian area of the Sikasso cercle, *Dyo* leaders set fire to one of the rolled up legs of their trousers and ran through tall dry grass setting it on fire.[16] Paques recorded a similar ritual in this area.[17]

Once the bush had been burned, sacrifices were made to the sacred stone and other ritual objects in the sanctuary, including the *Gouan* statues. These sacrifices marked the end of the retreat period for both *Dyo* and *Gouan* initiates. Those women who had previously been initiated into the *Dyo* because their parents lacked sons or because they were born out-of-wedlock were permitted access to the *Gouan* statues at this time for the purpose of making sacrifices to them. The *Dyo Sia* removed the statues from the sanctuary and placed them within the circular enclosure of brambles and trees that surrounded it. Sacrificial materials were either poured directly on the statues or in front of them but during other times they were poured on the door of the sanctuary.

During the latter days of their initiation, *Dyo* postulants were taught the dances and songs associated with *Dyo* public rituals and ceremonies by those who were already initiated, some of whom were themselves being initiated into the *Gouan*. This older generation of initiates also taught the postulants how to make the various costumes and headdresses and how to play the musical instruments. During this time, the initiates were divided by the *Dyo Sia* into the various groups of the society. With the advent of the tilling season, the initiation rites of both the *Dyo* and *Gouan* were temporarily suspended, to be resumed at the end of the harvesting period in October.

Once the harvest was in, the *Dyo Sia* removed the *Gouan* statues from the sanctuary. Women initiates came out to the enclosure where the statues were and decorated them with bits of cloth and colorful beads. They dusted them as well as rubbed them with shea butter. Ezra states that the women "washed" the statues.[18] French-speaking Bambara interpreters often use the word "laver" (wash) when "nettoyer" (clean) is

meant. This is because the latter is usually used to refer to the clearing of fields prior and during cultivation and not for conveying the notion of body cleaning. Were the statues washed with any kind of liquid, they could not acquire the sort of patina so many of them have. All of the numerous informants I questioned were unequivocal in stating that the statues were cleaned and never washed with any liquid. But, of course, there could have been exceptions to this.

The *Gouan* statues that had been readied in the sanctuary enclosure were then carried aloft in procession into the village at night by all the members of the *Gouan* and those undergoing initiation and placed in the vestibule of the *Dyo Sia's* house. For a period of seven days, the statues were taken out daily and public rituals and dances held in which only women initiates actively participated. Those men and women who had not undergone *Gouan* initiation were required to leave the village or stay indoors during some of these ceremonies.[19] *Dyo* postulants went outside of the village during the *Gouan* ceremonies, played their instruments and performed their dances and pantomimes.[20]

Travels of Initiates

The postulants of the various *Dyo* groups became itinerant for several weeks after the harvesting season. Their itineraries were not random affairs, but carefully planned trips that essentially took them to both near and distant villages where women from their village had married and settled. There was considerable variation in the number of villages visited. Paques for example recorded that the *N'Kenie* group of Sola visited nine villages in 1953; the *N'Tokofa* of Sola Sukuro, seven villages and the *N'Tokofa* of another village, twenty one villages.[21] Traveling *Dyo* groups were given presents in the villages they visited and had a license to steal certain food items such as peanuts and kola nuts. They put on musical and dance performances both in the villages they visited as well as enroute to them.[22]

N'Tokofa

Paques has presented a detailed description of the *N'Kenie, N'Tokofa* and *Dyoburu* societies.[23] The following comments are essentially a synthesis of her observations and my own. The *N'Tokofa,* as previously described, were buffoons, counterparts to the *Kwore Duga.* The total number of individuals in a village *Dyo* gorup was never great because of the limited number of initiates. This was especially true where initiation took place every three years as it did in some areas. Ideally, as Paques explains, an *N'Tokofa* group consisted of five principal people, four musicians and one singer. This ideal grouping, however, was not always achieved. The central figure was the *badia* (great mother) or (great goat) who represented a nanny goat. The player depicted goodness, concern and patience. The counter figure was the *badeni* (small child), representing an undisciplined and unruly baby goat. There were two twin figures, *sumadie* (white platter) and the *sumafin* (black platter). The former represented a good man, the latter a mean one. The fifth principal member of the troupe was the *dyeli,* the singer or bard who was responsible for presiding over sacrifices for the group. The *dyeli* carried the group's talismans and wore a fiber cape to which he attached sticks representing the villages visited. When the number of *N'Tokofa* initiates was large, the remainder comprised various categories of buffoons. There were considerable temporal and geographic variations in these. Paques recorded several, *benzema* (opportunist), *diara dia* (big lion), *sokoro* (frightening one), *diama kunko* (he who concerns everyone) and *serebu.* I recorded *zantegeba* (big handed one), *wara ba* (big animal) and *kilisi tigui* (chief of testicular hairs).

All of the buffoons of the *N'Tokofa* wore cotton trousers, the left legs of which were shorter than the right. Paques recorded that these trousers were yellow in color, but sometimes they were white as well. They also wore vests made from blackened *n'teke* (*Cordia mixa*) fibers and elaborate skirts of yellow colored wild baobab fibers (*koroforo*) held in place by belts made from red and white *nere* fibers (*Parkia biglobosa*).

The *N'Tokofa* bards wore a large cape of yellow colored wild baobab fibers and carried five fly whisks made from *tume* fibers (*Strycnos spinosa*). The most dramatic aspect of *N'Tokofa* costumes was the headdress. Buffoons wore the dried heads and wings of various large birds including hornbills, ducks, falcons, vultures, etc. These were attached to wigs of yellow colored wild baobab fibers and held in place as were the birds by *nere* fibers. As Paques recorded, the *badeni* and *sumafin* buffoons each carried a yellow sac used for holding the troupe's gifts and its roan antelope horn which was one of its musical instruments. The buffoons also carried small calabashes covered with nets to which seeds were attached. These calabashes made a rattling noise when played. It is important to note that such calabashes were not unique to the *Dyo,* but widely used in Bambara country. Their other musical instruments were bells and irons whose serrated edges were rubbed with another iron.

N'Kenie

N'Kenie membership was also a reflection of the total numbers of *Dyo* initiates. Paques for example found eleven members of the Sola village group in 1953. Eight carried drums, two were dancers and one mimed a female role. Most *N'Kenie* groups I investigated had either seven or eight drums. Extra initiates were accommodated as dancers or mimers. Some groups had fewer than seven drums.

The costuming of *N'Kenie* troupes was in some ways much more elaborate than that of *N'Tokofa.* As Paques has described, all members wore skirts made from blackened baobab fibers. The members who carried the sculpted drums plus the bard also wore an underskirt of blackened and plaited *n'teke* fibers. They did not wear anything on their heads whereas the bard and the others wore wigs which simulated the hair styles of Bambara women of long ago. All members of the troupe wore simple or elaborate chest coverings decorated with red and white *nere* beads.

Additional elements of *N'Kenie* costuming and their religious symbolism have been described in great detail by Paques.[24] Of particular interest to the focus of this discussion were the headdresses worn by the two principal members of the troupe. The *n'keniamba,* the leader of the troupe, who carried the large drums of the same name wore a sculpted wooden headdress in the form of a semi-circle representing a rainbow. The second most important figure in the *N'Kenie* troupe, the *tium,* also wore a sculpted wooden headdress with three points representing a cock's comb. This symbolized the cock who is master of the seventh heaven.[25] The *N'Kenie* bard also wore a wooden headdress symbolizing the rainbow. Female initiates of both the *N'Tokofa* and the *N'Kenie* wore costumes that differed slightly from male members. They did not assume pivotal roles however in these groups.

Musical Instruments of the *N'Kenie*

There were essentially eight canoe shaped drums used by *N'Kenie* groups. The largest and most important was the *n'keniamba* which in some villages measured four feet long. It and the other drums had serrated sides, were hollowed out and had a conical foot support at the base. The *n'keniamba* was considered the mother of the other drums and set the rhythm for them.[26] The next drum was called *tium* and was considered masculine. Drums of this type measured about two feet or so in length and frequently had a sculpted head or torso at the top end. The third most important drum was the *tierum.* It was also considered masculine and was sculpturally similar to the *tium* except that it was smaller. The next two drums were used by the bard and the troupe's treasurer respectively and were considered masculine *tiums.* The next two drums were called *fere* and were considered as *tiums* and frequently as one drum as well. The least important drum and the smallest was the *moyo-moyo*, representing a shamed and disorganized male.[27] The drums of the *N'Kenie* were really not drums in the strictest sense but rattles since their serrated sides were rubbed with sticks. The stick of a given drum was attached to a cord which in turn was threaded through a hole in the bottom of the drum and then knotted. Except for the *n'keniamba,* the drums were cradled in the left arm and usually only one side rubbed with the stick. Paques relates that in the Sikasso area the drums were made by blacksmiths from kapock (*Bombax buonopozense*), but that in Sokura from *Sterculia tamentosa* (*koroba*), or from *Styrchnos spinosa.*[28] There were departures from these woods with *Bombax costatum* (*dioum*) being used occasionally and other woods as well.

All of the *N'Kenie* drums were sculpted by blacksmiths and were communal village property. They were passed on from one generation of initiates to another. Costumes for all *Dyo* groups however were discarded by initiates after their iniation was over.

The *n'keniamba* drums had sculpted human heads which lacked mouths but which had longitudinal crowns passing from the forehead to the nape of the neck. There were two holes at the bottom of these drums for the ropes that were used to carry them. The player of the *n'keniamba* carried several hard wood sticks with which to play the instrument. Paques recorded that eight sticks were used, but in a number of villages I investigated the number was said to be variable.

Dyoburu

Dyoburu groups were not as numerous as *N'Tokofa* and *N'Kenie* ones. And generally few were found in villages that possessed *N'Tokofa* or *N'Kenie*. Paques in documenting a group in the village of Kouroulamini found that it possessed nine trumpets (horns).[29] In other villages, I surveyed, the number of trumpets never exceeded nine, but were frequently fewer than six. Essentially, these were of four types. The largest, *buruba* (mother trumpet), had a sculpted head surmounted by two long horns at one extremity. The next two trumpets were considered twins and were architectonically similar to the *buruba* except that the sculpted heads were devoid of facial features. The next pair, also considered twins, differed from the preceding pair in that one horn emerged from the sculpted head instead of two. There then came three trumpets considered triplets that were similar to the previous pair. And finally the smallest trumpet had a truncated sculpted horn at one end.[30]

Dyoburu horns are often wrongly identified as *Komo* society trumpets, known as *buru sama* (elephant trumpet). Such trumpets, however, are made of iron, whereas the *dyoburu* ones are sculpted from wood. In terms of design, *buru sama* resemble some *dyoburu* because like them they have two horns at one end. These two horns represent the jaws of the crocodile that imprison the cock's spur that contains *korte*, a material element used in sorcery. In order to understand this sculptural symbolism, one must be familiar with the traditional Bambara religious beliefs which they reflect. The traditional Bambara believed in the existence of seven heavens connected to earth by the branches of the *bana* tree (*Ceiba pentandra*). It was via these heavens and the branches of this tree that ancestor spirits descended to earth. Inversely, sacrifices made by men ascend to ancestral spirits via the tree and the seven heavens. A white cock was the master of the seventh heaven. His sounds were benedictions that generated earthly fertility. They traveled down through the six other heavens, bringing to earth the beneficial powers of these celestial levels as well. Because of the special place of the white cock in Bambara cosmology, the sacrifice of this animal was considered among the most powerful that could be made.

Of interest is the fact that *Komo* society members often used cock spurs as containers for powerful poisons made from plants. The opening of the spur was sealed with bee's wax. When a *korte*, which could be sent at great distances, was desired, the wax plug was pierced with a metal hook which itself had been immersed in viper venom, and the spur pointed in the direction of the desired victim.[31] Even among Islamized Bambara today, there is a strong belief in *korte* which are perceived as material elements of sorcery that can travel great distances to penetrate the skins of victims.[32] The crocodile was believed a powerful supernatural force whose powers

were used for divination and for countering sorcery. It was symbolically portrayed on door locks for example as a triangular head design, now interpreted by Moslem Bambara as representing a male ancestor. Its open jaws were also portrayed on door locks as two horn like structures emanating from the head of a human form. These jaws were symbolically poised to capture *korte*. In recent years, Moslem Bambara have interpreted the architectonics of such locks as representing the ears of the *Kono*, which hears all or the ears of the *Komo* who knows all.[33] The older symbolism, however, was closer to the traditional Bambara religion.

The other musical instruments used by *Dyoburu* were calabashes and drums. The former were identical to those used by *N'Tokofa* and the latter were the well known *jembe* variety which have a narrow lower portion that is inserted between the legs of the player.

Other Groups

Blacksmiths had their own special groups, not really perceived as an integral part of the *Dyo*. It was called the *Numu Dyo* or the *N'Keribadjo*.[34] It was also referred to as the *Duga* in many villages I investigated, but was essentially extinct as was the *M'Para Sien* and the *Soma* about which no meaningful details could be obtained. The *Basso* was a group that used iron bells but it was extinct by the 1960's.

Public Performances

N'Kenie and *N'Tokofa* groups from the same village usually traveled together through the countryside and simultaneously visited the same locales. When an *N'Kenie* group performed on a village square, its members marched to it in a predictable order first recorded by Paques. Two dancers led the group tracing a line on the ground symbolizing the form of the mythical *bana* tree. Then came the eight drummers and finally the bard carrying a wooden female statue, the *Nyeni* (little girl) or *Dyonyeni.* Statues of this genre measure about eighteen inches high. During dances, they were mimed to convey a variety of meanings or placed standing on the ground. Other *Dyo* groups such as the blacksmiths also possessed similar statues. Frequently groups had more than one statue. Some informants stated that the *Dyonyeni* represented female *N'Kenie* members who did not as a rule travel with the group. Others said these statues were simply female companions of *N'Kenie* groups.

Paques recorded that *N'Kenie* groups performed two types of dances, the *kile kile m'buo* (one to one dance) and the *fla fla do* (two to two dance). The former was perfomed during the rainy season in the home village throughout the initial period of initiation. The latter was the dance performed by intinerant groups. The chief characteristics of this dance as described to me in the field by informants consisted of the drummers slowly moving around in a circle. The bard moved around the circle in the opposite direction while singing and holding the Dyonyeni statue. The dancers danced at four corners around the circle and then moved around counter to the direction of the drummers. Paques recorded that the *n'keniamba* drummer then broke out of the circle and moved around it with the bard.[35] The *moyo-moyo* then disrupted this cadence by changing to a rapid rhythm, putting himself into direct conflict with the pace setting *n'keniamba*. The circular dance disrupted, the dancers restored order by retracing the chevrons of the mythical *bana* tree with their dance steps.[36] The *n'keniamba* drummer then started the rhythm for the circular dance once again. Finally the performance ended with everyone remaining still while the drummers rattled a rapid beat. Paques cogently observed that the movement of the drummers was in the direction of nocturnal stellar movement.[37]

N'Tokofa performances resembled those of *N'Kenie* in that circular movement was central to the choreography. The buffoons danced in a circle while the sumafin blew his horn. The bard moved around the outside of the circle in the opposite direction, stopping

at the supposed cardinal points. A number of these bards carried sculpted wooden crocodiles, which were antisorcery symbols. Paques does not mention them, probably because their use was neither consistent nor widespread. The *N'Tokofa* performed a second dance for which the calabashes and the iron rod of the *badeni* provided the music.[38]

When *N'Kenie* and *N'Tokofa* groups performed together, as they often did, their dances represented integrated versions of what has just been described. The words to the songs sung by both these groups were both comical and obscene. Paques relates that many of them dealt with food but informants related that they also focused on sexual themes. The words were uttered amidst the din of the music and were thus difficult for spectators to hear and understand. But initiates knew full well what they were saying.

Other Rituals

Aside from the public manifestations of the *Dyo* and *Gouan,* there were regular private rituals presided over by the *Dyo Sia.* Funeral ceremonies of *Dyo Sia* were especially important rituals. It was during these rituals and the initiation rites of both societies that elaborate iron staffs were used. These staffs were often topped by male or female human figures, bearing a striking resemblance to the wooden *Gouan* statues. Some staffs contained numerous bell shaped rattles. Both societies used iron lamps (*fitine*), often surmounted by human iron figures. Not all Bambara lamps, however, fall into this category. Many were simply utilitarian objects used to light the interiors of homes.

Elaborate funeral ceremonies were held not only for *Dyo Sia* but also for female leaders of the *Gouan.* Informants stated that ritual irons were used during both types of ceremonies. During these rites some of the irons were placed standing in the ground beneath the village's *bana* tree, while others were actually attached to the lower branches of the tree. It should be recalled that the traditional Bambara believed that the souls of the deceased and sacrifices to ancestors ascend the branches of the bana in order to gain access to the seven heavens and the after-life. During some parts of these funeral rites, these irons were carried as wands or high in the air as display sculptures.

During initiation rites of both the *Dyo* and *Gouan* these irons were also placed stand-ing in the ground in the sacred grove where the sanctuary was located. Some were also at-tached to the branches of the inner ring of trees of the grove.

A question that I frequently put to in-formants was what distinguishes a *Dyo* staff from a *Gouan* one. In some villages, the staffs were viewed as belonging to either one or the other. Such affiliation was defined in terms of who had ordered and paid for the staff and vertical descent from previous cohorts of initi-ates. In other villages this distinction did not exist, the staffs being used simultaneously and interchangeably by both groups. There was good but not complete correlation between perceptions of *Gouan* separateness from the *Dyo* and segregation of iron staff use.

When shown photographs of staffs with sculpted *Gouan* figures on them, most in-fomants categorized them as *Gouan* staffs. Although informants were able to provide interpretation of the symbolism of other iron staffs, frequently they could not categorize them as uniquely belonging to one or the other group. Thus if it is not possible for *Dyo* and *Gouan* members to deduce iron staff af-filiation from visual evidence alone, except for the ones with *Gouan* figures, it is impos-sible for western African art experts to do so either. Consequently, except where a staff clearly depicts *Gouan* figures, one cannot come to a definitive conclusion about its con-textual use. In view of the fact that so many *Gouan* groups were considered by initiates themselves to be part of the *Dyo*, one could consider most of these irons as *Dyo* staffs.

Ritual and Functional Roles of Women

The role of women in both the *Dyo* and *Gouan* represents something of a dramatic departure when viewed against the back-ground of other Bambara initiation societies which were male dominated. Of course, women had their own societies, some of which still function today.[39] Yet throughout the complex of male dominated *dyow* no-where did women play so significant a role as they did in the *Dyo* and *Gouan*, and especially in the latter.

The female membership of the *Dyo* con-sisted of two types of women, those born out of wedlock and those without brothers. Where a corresponding *Gouan* group existed, these women inherited ritual leadership roles and as such were called *massa*. Interestingly, such ritual leadership in the *Gouan* did not carry with it functional leadership. While these two categories of young girls were being initiated into the *Dyo*, their female counter-parts were being directly inducted into the *Gouan* along with the next older generation of males and those older girls who had already passed through the *Dyo*. Thus *Dyo* passage was required of girls seen as representing *Nyale's* disordered creative processes before they could enter the *Gouan*. Also, the entry of a younger age grade of girls simultaneously with an older age grade of males demon-strated the overwhelmingly female orientation of the *Gouan*. There were of course numerous variations in the initiation process just out-lined, many of these emerging in the late years of these two societies when traditional Bambara society in general began to break-down.

Functional leadership in the *Gouan* rested with women whose talents and abilities enabled them to acquire certain kinds of knowledge and skills. Although blacksmiths were excluded from membership in *Dyo* groups, their wives were not excluded from *Gouan* membership. Excision, which generally accompanied *Gouan* entry was frequently but not exclusively performed by these women. *Maniamaga mousso*, traditional Bambara mid-wives, held functional leadership roles in the *Gouan* because of their acquired knowledge not only about childbirth, but about a host of women's concerns. These include fertility, menstruation, pregnancy, lactation, nutrition and general health in addition to larger non-medical social concerns. Through these women, female *Gouan* members had access to non-exploitative fee for service medical care that had traditional legitimacy. In some respects this is similar to the situation that exists in the *Sande* society of Sierra Leone.[40] *Maniamaga mousso* are not just midwives. Rather they are broader versed and skilled traditional medical practitioners whose knowledge of herbs enables them to deal with a wide range of medical problems in women. Through them women have access to a referral system of other practitioners, consisting of both men and women.

The funerals of *massa* and other prominent senior women of the *Gouan* were elaborate affairs during which irons and wooden statues were carried aloft from the sanctuary in procession to the village. Such processions also took place during times of *Dyo* and *Gouan* initiation and during the funerals of *Dyo Sia*. Some informants reported that the statues were not held aloft except when they were being carried to and from the village along with the irons for initiation and funeral rites. Others stated that the irons and the statues were also carried aloft as display sculptures during public initiation and funeral dances. Clearly there were both area and temporal differences in this practice.

In studying the Fodonon group of Senufo in nearby northern Ivory Coast, Anita Glaze found that similar statues were used as display sculptures and carried aloft by the Women's *Poro* during funeral rituals held in honor of senior *Tyekpa* society women.[41]

The Nature of the *Gouan*

As previously mentioned, the Bambara had a number of women's societies, some of which still function. Unfortunately, few of these societies were ever studied by social scientists and studies conducted today may not tell us much about their nature and functions several decades ago. Some of these societies, such as the *Nya Goua* and the *Mousso Ka Dyiri* have an exclusively female membership. Yet they are connected to the world of men by blacksmiths in the case of

the former and by other men in the case of the latter. Other societies like the *Gouan* had both male and female members. The pattern of mixed membership separates the *Gouan* from societies like *Mousso Ka Dyiri*. But it makes it more akin to the *Dyo* in this regard with which it was intimately related.

The *Mousso Ka Dyiri* once functioned along the middle Bani, just to the north and east of the *Gouan*. It was still functioning in the late 1960's when I was able to observe it in several villages in what was then the Koutiala cercle, now the Bla cercle. It was in a sense a sister society to the *Gouan*, present where the *Dyo* counterpart, the *Kwore* was also found. This society was first described as long ago as 1910 by Father Henry.[42] He found that it was not present in all villages and that its membership was confined to excised unmarried women. While the latter characterization was true of initiates, I found that there was a hierarchy within the society that included married women as well.

The material altar of the *Mousso Ka Dyiri* in each village was a tree closely situated next to the village wall. Often it was a *toro* tree (*Ficus vogeli*). Henry reported this in 1910 and sixty years later I found it still to be the case. In some villages in the M'pessoba area I found that women entered and left villages next to the trees, touching them as they did so. Henry reported that the women of this society held dances on the night of a new moon to the accompaniment of a drum, the *mousso denou*.[43] Few men observed these dances which he characterized as indecent. Henry also reported that an annual dance ceremony was held beneath the tree during which a blood sacrifice was rubbed on the trunk.[44] These ritual patterns were still being observed in 1970. Interestingly, many men and even outside male interpreters were fearful of approaching these trees at that time. The *Mousso Ka Dyiri* was also a mutual aid society that like age group associations came to the assistance of members when needed. The head of the society was generally an old woman. Henry observed that it was usually the oldest woman in the village.[45] But I found this to be variable. Of interest is the fact that the woman leader of a village chapter was called *massa*, a title used for women in leadership positions in the *Gouan*.

The goal of the *Mousso Ka Dyiri* was to insure the onset of menses in young girls, normal lactation and pregnancy.[46] Informants told me that in addition the society protected women against adultery on the part of their husbands and made them attractive to their spouses as well. Thus the society was focused on women's concerns.

Henry noted that during the society's dances, members lifted their breasts to the tree and rubbed their umbilici on its trunk. He concluded that young women did so to develop breasts and married women to maintain or increase their fertility.[47] Both also did so to protect themselves from the evils to which women were susceptible.[48] Annual festivals were very grand affairs and as Henry describes, beer and millet porridge were made by the society's members and given to all the men of the village. In addition, kola nuts were given to family heads and to some other males in the village.[49]

The annual sacrifices made to the tree consisted of cereal porridge, a chicken and kola nuts. Significantly while women members made the non-blood sacrifices themselves, the village chief or another male elder was called upon to make the blood sacrifice.[50] Thus men served in the crucial role of intermediary between women members and the protector spirit represented by the tree. This protector spirit was said by some to be a collectivity of ancestral women spirits. Others, however, saw it as an elaboration of *Dassiri* which are village protector spirits, but particularized for women. Interestingly, some informants said it represented *Mousso Koroni* and *Ndomadyiri,* powerful joint architects of progressive creation. Such an interpretation, given by old knowledgeable women and men, provokes interest because these two powerful supernatural beings are seen by some as the center of the *Gouan* cult.

As is the case with the *Mousso Ka Dyiri*, the *Gouan* has multiple symbolic meanings, depending on the participant's perspective and level of knowledge. Both societies dealt with women's concerns and both were linked to the world of men by intermediaries. Yet the *Gouan*, unlike the *Mousso Ka Dyiri*, had a mixed male and female membership. In this regard it mirrored the larger *Dyo* grouping to which it was connected in various ways.

In the area of its southern distribution, the *Gouan* was seen by highly knowledgeable informants as a cult centered on a specific post-creation ancestor, namely *Gouandousou* and to a lesser extent on her husband, *Gouantigui.* Less knowledgeable informants shared this view. However, in the northern area, highly informed individuals saw the *Gouan* as a cult devoted to two principal supernatural personalities, prominent in the myth of creation (See Chapter 3). These individuals are *Mousso Koroni* (*Nyale*) and *Ndomadyiri*. In this area people used the names *Mousso Koroni* and *Nyale* interchangeably, although the latter more accurately refers to *Mousso Koroni* in the present third phase of creation. The cult appealed to *Mousso Koroni*, a powerful creative force, the mistress of sorcery, the source of all fertility and courage. It also appealed to *Ndomadyiri,* the divine blacksmith, who gives order to *Mousso Koroni's* creative processes. He is the great stabilizer in the world, the healer and master of herbal medicine.

Less informed individuals in the northern area viewed the *Gouan* as an ancestor cult, devoted to ancestors in general but to none in particular. Thus in the areas where the *Gouan* existed, it was simultaneously viewed in three different ways, as a general ancestor cult, as a specific ancestor cult and as a cult devoted to two powerful creative supernatural beings.

Although the *Gouan* was greatly concerned with human fertility and procreation it had other areas of concern as well. It focused on agricultural fertility whose source is *Mousso Koroni*. It addressed male concerns as well, sexual potency, physical attractiveness and strength and offspring. In a sense it complemented the *Dyo* which focused on agricultural fertility.

Ezra who conducted field research in Mali in 1978 in areas where the *Gouan* once existed, characterizes it as a fertility cult. She reports that the *Gouan* cult and its statues helped infertile women have children.[51] She also reports that people familiar with *Gouan* statues claim that they do not represent mythological or historical persons.[52] She goes on to say that the female statues take their meaning from the roles of women within the *Gouan* fertility cult.

As explained above, it is not surprising that a number of Bambara would not see the *Gouan* statues as representing mythological persons, namely *Mousso Koroni* and *Ndomadyiri* or historical persons namely *Gouandousou* and *Gouantigui*. However, none of my informants saw the primary symbolism of the female statues as reflective of the role of women in either the cult or in Bambara society at large. For them these statues represent either *Mousso Koroni* the supernatural female creator, *Gouandousou* the gifted and powerful historical figure or female ancestors as a collectivity. Ezra's field observation is an extremely important one because it demonstrates yet another level of interpretation. At this level the female statues portray a woman's ideal status and role in Bambara society, as a mother, as pregnant, as possessing lactating breasts and as engaged in such female labor tasks as carrying water in a jar above her head.

Chapter 5

The Art and Its Meaning

The *Dyo* and *Gouan* societies used a remarkable array of representational art objects in their ceremonies. But because of the limited geographic distribution of these societies and the custom of inter-generational transfer of objects, total numbers are few. Indeed, these objects are relatively rare in western museum and private collections.

Iron Staffs and Figures

The contextual uses of iron staffs by both the *Dyo* and *Gouan* have already been discussed. In addition, small iron figures were also used, but only in a shrine context. The architectonics of the human figures on some iron staffs closely resemble those of wooden *Gouan* statuary. These staffs were used by *Gouan* initiates and indeed some of the Bambara say that those with female figures on them symbolize *Gouandousou* while those with male figures symbolize *Gouantigui*. Other Bambara see *Mousso Koroni* (*Nyale*) and *Ndomadyiri* respectively represented in such irons while others see them as symbolic of female and male ancestors.

Other staffs, embellished with bell like bits of iron were usually used by non-*Gouan* groups of the *Dyo*. Most iron sculptures were regularly sprinkled with libations of millet beer and millet porridge. Of significance is the fact that the human figures in *Gouan* iron staffs are frequently sexually distinguishable. This does not usually hold true, however, for Dogon iron staff figures. It is important to note that iron figures were by no means limited to the *Dyo* and *Gouan* societies among the Bambara. For example, the Samake Bambara people of Bougouni once used small iron horsemen as ancestral grave markers. These iron figures, seen in the field by Paques in 1952, measured about twenty centimeters in height.[1] During the 1960's and 1970's, a number of contemporary irons of this genre were mass produced just across the river from Bamako, Mali's capital, and sold on the local art market. They have now found their way into a number of private and museum collections.

Gouan iron figures, whether they be on lamps (*fitine*) or on staffs (*bisa nege*), often have large spreading hands which informants relate represent the feet of the crocodile. These figures sometimes display stylized conical hats, called *bamada* (crocodile mouth). Such hats were once commonly worn by Bambara elders and symbolized the power of the crocodile's mouth in destroying *korte* (sorcery substance). Other figures display the three braided hair style that was also once common among the Bambara. Significantly, Bambara men used to braid their hair as well. By the 1960's this practice was rare except in isolated areas such as Sarro, Beledougou and the Kaarta. The facial features of most irons are generally indistinct, probably because of age. The flap of the *bamada* sometimes flares out at the nape of the neck, representing a crocodile's tail.

The iron staffs of both the *Dyo* and *Gouan* are referred to by a variety of names, including *nege, bisa nege, kala nege* and *sono*. As a group, these staffs ultimately represent the serpent, the symbol of light, progressive creation, and time as perceived by the Bambara. Seasons are not viewed by them as different periods of time, but rather as aspects of the same time.[2] The snake symbol, besides having a close relationship with the concept of time, also has one with agriculture. As the snake undergoes periodic moults and sheds its skin, so does the earth, the farmer causing the earth to moult when he tills the soil. As the snake remains the same after each moult so too does the earth after each harvest.[3]

Also symbolized in some irons is *Mousso Koroni's* relationships with the spitting cobra by whom she conceived and gave birth to *Tyi Wara* who invented agriculture. Sometimes, iron staffs depict a trident of serpents. These are said to symbolize the triple python who represents a continuous route of fertility. The trident, as explained by Paques, is the second sign that came forth out of *Bemba*, the first human ancestor.[4] While the sign of the serpent alone represents the progression of life, the twisting of the serpent symbolizes life's transformations. This too is depicted in some irons.

Thus the irons of both the *Dyo* and the *Gouan* incorporate within them all of the symbolic meanings of the serpent. To these meanings are added others, symbolized by figures such as *Gouandousou* which represents fertility and creation and a powerful force against malevolent sorcery.

Wooden Hoes and Wooden Swords

Two *Dyo* objects that are extremely rare in collections are wooden hoes and wooden swords that were both shrine and display objects. Both were often completely sculpted from wood and the former were sometimes decorated with a human head at the junction of the handle and the wooden blade. The *Kwore Duga* buffoons of the *Kwore* society usually carried wooden swords and the *Tyi Wara* society used wooden hoes as display objects. Consequently, it is difficult and perhaps impossible to categorize objects in collections as belonging to one or the other of these societies without knowing their actual contextual use.

The heads on the hoes of both the *Dyo* and the *Tyi Wara* sometimes show the stylized hooded neck of the spitting cobra (*Naja nigricollis*). This snake has a direct relationship with agriculture in Bambara mythology (Chapter 3), and along with other snakes is intimately connected to both agricultural and human fertility. One could cogently argue that primarily agricultural societies elaborated such symbolic roles for snakes given the significant danger they pose to farmers. Indeed, the *Tyi Wara* society, when it was in full vigor, was from a certain perspective a snake cult. Its members captured snakes as part of their annual ceremonies, ate some of them,

used others ritually and prepared anti-venom which they made available to the entire community.[5] The leaders of the *Tyi Wara* were still feared in the late 1960's for their knowledge of snake venoms even though the society was almost extinct in most areas. During that period, many Bambara still feared them because of their alleged ability to use snake venom for poisoning people and for making *korte* (sorcery substance).

N'Kenie Drums and *Dyoburu* Trumpets

The symbolic meanings and other information about these objects have already been presented in some detail in Chapter 4. It is worth noting, however, that *N'Kenie* drums are among the rarest of Bambara art objects. This derives from their use in a limited number of villages, since not all villages that practiced the *Dyo* necessarily had an *N'Kenie* group, and from the fact that they were passed on from one generation of initiates to the next. *N'Kenie* drums were also subject to rather intense physical use. In the later years of the *Dyo* society, *N'Kenie* members whose drums had broken tended not to have them replaced with new ones. Rather they simply carried on with fewer drums. The old ones were left to rot in the village shrine.

Although the total number of *Dyoburu* trumpets in existence at one time was probably not much different from the numbers of *N'Kenie* drums, these instruments were not subject to intense physical use. Fewer of them broke and so a large number of them survived to find their way into western art collections.

Gouandousou Statues

The most dramatic objects of the *Dyo* and *Gouan*, in addition to the *N'Kenie* drums, are the *Gouan* statues. Thematically, these statues fall into several main groups, including seated women with children, seated or standing women with pregnant abdomens, standing women without pregnant abdomens and men, either standing, seated or on horseback. Within all of these groups there are stylistic variations. The best known theme perhaps is the seated mother and child. Statues of this genre have frequently been referred to by westerners as "queens," a concept not far from the Bambara view of them. The Bambara refer to them as *Gouandousou,* the name being derived from *dousou,* meaning passionate ardor, courage, desire, source of passions and *gouan* which among other things means hot.

Those Bambara who believe that *Gouandousou* is a legendary ancestor state that her courage was greater than that of men, as great as that of the finest hunters and talisman makers. Thus they say, for this reason, some statues show *Gouandousou* wearing a hat decorated with talismans, an article of attire usually reserved for powerful men. Statues that depict this hat in effect announce *Gouandousou's* supernatural powers and her social position as an equal of male leaders. The latter attribute is sometimes symbolized by an arm dagger and by the depiction of knife and dagger points on the hat. Others see the talismans on the hat as being cock's spurs, the spurs of the cock of the seventh heaven, filled with sorcery substance, hence endowed with enormous power. Some see animal claws in these forms which protect against *nyama,* the powerful spiritual force of all things which on the death of an animal roams free. *Nyama* can cause illness and misfortune. On some statues there is an arching crest, which although resembling an abstract depiction of the *bamada* hat, is said by some informants to rerpresent the rainbow. They correctly point out that such crests were once worn by some *N'Kenie* members. Such crests, sculpted from wood, were also worn in the southern area of the *Gouan* by some of the *Gouan* membership. The rainbow not only points to the place where the supreme being is at a given moment, but is also the site of the celestial *bana* tree (*Ceiba pentandra*). In the cosmology of the ancient Bambara, it is by the branches of this tree that the spirits of the deceased ascend through seven heavens to the supreme being. They also descend to earth from these heavens via the branches of this tree. Through this symbolism, *Gouandousou*

is depicted as being in contact not only with powerful ancestral spirits but also with the supreme being.

In some villages there were accounts of *Gouandousou's* specific accomplisments and deeds and her powers against witchcraft and sorcery. Of interest is the fact that a number of these accomplishments are similar to the creative acts attributed to *Mousso Koroni* in the myth of creation believed by other Bambara people to the north. Yet the Bambara who see *Gouandousou* as a legendary ancestor see her as having powers to protect them against sorcery which was initially created by *Mousso Koroni.* At first glance this may seem incongruous because *Gouandousou* herself was a powerful sorceress. But to understand this one must look at it the way the ancient Bambara did. It is only by possessing sorcery powers that one can truly be an anti-sorcerer as well. By worshiping *Gouandousou,* the ancient Bambara in effect requested that she use both her sorcery and anti-sorcery powers on their behalf. It is important to understand that the ancient Bambara viewed sorcery as a principal cause for infertility, and saw sorcery as a powerful tool for achieving good ends as well as evil ones.

In other areas of the southern Bambara country, people view *Gouandousou* not as a specific ancestor, but as representing ancestral women in general. She embodies not only them, but also all their collective powers. In other areas, as already described in Chapter 3, *Gouandousou* statues are said to represent *Mousso Koroni,* the first sorcerer, the first creative force on earth and *Nyale,* as *Mousso Koroni* is known in her second coming so to speak, in the present third phase of creation. In this phase she is the source of all activity and animation.

If this symbolism be so, I often inquired of informants, then why are not the statues called *Mousso Koroni* or *Nyale.* Their answer was unexpected. They said that there was no need to have a statue of *Faro* because his presence was understood. *Nyale* and *Ndomadyiri* could not function, could not exist in the world without the presence of *Faro.* Thus as they saw it there was no need to spell out the presence of this, the most powerful of the original creative supernatural beings. In a sense this reply answered my question because if *Faro* were not depicted in sculpture then *Mousso Koroni* (*Nyale*) and *Ndomadyiri*, the lesser deities who were, did not have to be mentioned by name.

Before going on with a further analysis of the architectonics of *Gouandousou* statues and their symbolism it is well to briefly review what has already been written about these statues. The seated mother and child figures first appeared on the western African art market in the late 1950's. By this time both the *Dyo* and *Gouan* had already ceased to function in a number of villages and the objects once sacred to these groups were often no longer protected. In addition, their continued presence constituted a point of friction with a young rising Moslem power structure insecure about itself and its future. There were ready buyers for these and other *Gouan* and *Dyo* objects among the field agents of a couple of Bamako based Moslem art dealers. And local youths often entered into collusion with such agents to steal those objects still fiercely guarded by ageing *Dyo Sia*. The Bamako dealers, who had begun their dealerships soon after World War II, had long since established regular commercial links with Parisian dealers, some of whom regularly visited Bamako. But more often than not, it was the Bamako dealers who traveled up to Paris with art objects, in order to return with much desired western manufacturers.[6] Both the Bamako and Parisian dealers may have known something about the six principal Bambara *dyow* and the art objects associated with them, but they were almost totally ignorant about the *Dyo* and *Gouan*.[7] These societies had no counterparts among the majority of the Bambara so that even knowledgeable African dealers in Bamako could not integrate the fragmentary information their field agents brought them. And these agents themselves, not being natives of the southern Bambara country had no frame of reference for whatever was told them.[8] Until this present communication no substantial contextual information has been published about the *Gouan*. And thus these statues have remained somewhat of an enigma

for both collectors and scholars.

In 1960, Robert Goldwater, then Director of the Museum of Primitive Art in New York City, wrote a brief description of these statues in a catalogue that accompanied the museum's exhibition, *Bambara Sculpture From The Western Sudan*. In it he said, "Recently, a number of larger figures . . . have been discovered around, and to the northwest of Bougouni. Most of them are women, portrayed standing or seated on low stools with a short, open back rest, and sometimes carrying an infant who clings to the mother's body. Particularly striking is the headdress, built up to a crest on the axis of the figure, and falling in several braids, or strands around the neck, sometimes low enough nearly to touch the prominent breasts . . . The female figures have been referred to as queens, and it has been suggested that they are type-portraits, much like those of the Bushongo kings. Their attitudes and attributes certainly suggest high rank of some sort, and they may indeed portray . . . chief's wives, but be ancestral figures of a more generalized kind."[9] Goldwater went on to say that these statues might perhaps fuse with the role of fertility figure and embody extension and overlapping of meanings.[10]

The first description of these statues and their contextual background based on field research was published in 1974.[11] Although brief, it essentially characterized the *Gouan* cult as one focused on fertility and the female statues as representing a mythical ancestor, *Gouandousou,* whose enormous magical powers were symbolized by the depiction of hats bearing talismans and charms. Such hats are frequently worn by hunters who are also *basitigui* (charm makers) and healers. While the *Dyo* placed a sharp focus on agricultural fertility, the *Gouan* placed it on human fertility. Thus it was that the latter's powers were especially invoked on behalf of women who were either childless or who had a variety of menstrual or lactation problems.

Ezra, who studied the *Gouan* in the field in 1978, essentially characterized it as a fertility cult whose primary purpose was to assist infertile women to have children. She states that women would promise that if they had a child, they would reward the cult with a sacrifice and name the child after one of the two principal statues.[12] I found no evidence during my field studies that women named children after *Gouan* statues. If this did occur, it was not a widespread practice. Children were and still are named after *Dassiri*, village protector spirits, materialized as trees, mountains, rocks, etc. Throughout the Bambara country, women frequently offer sacrifices to *Dassiri* in order to have children. And they sometimes promise to name future children after the *Dassiri* whatever the sex.

Ezra relates that the most important statues were the seated mothers with babies (*Gwandusu*) and their male counterparts (*Gwanjaraba*). She goes on to say that to this central couple were added a variety of other figures, who can be viewed as attendants.[13] Ezra's informants told her that none of the *Gouan* statues represented mythological or historical persons (See Chapter 4).

Ezra made an extremely important observation about *Gouan* statues in noting that many of them do not fit the stereotype of Bambara art. Instead of exhibiting the flat planes, sharp angles and pure geometric forms so classical of Bambara art as we know it, these statues are softly rounded, naturalistic and endowed with numerous and elaborate signs of rank.[14] It almost appears that these statues descend from another art tradition or else represent a major parallel style line that branched off from some primordial style in the distant past.

Gouandousou statues are frequently seated figures of women holding one or two children. The latter are extremely rare. Usually the single child is held closely, facing the mother's abdomen. Seated statues without children often manifest pregnant abdomens. In some statues the two side tresses descend down on to the breasts while a third tress falls down on the back. Statues manifesting these coiffure characteristics come from the northern area of *Gouan* distribution near the town of Dioila and constitute a "northern style."

In other *Gouandousou* statues, the two side tresses are spike-like, not descending on to the breasts. These statues constitute a

"southern style" being from the area between the towns of Bougouni and Sikasso.

Gouandousou statues vary in height from about 30 inches to 50 inches. There are rarely some that are taller than this. The color and patina of the wood is blonde, gray, brown or black, with or without evidence of sacrificial material. The stools on which the statues are seated are quite low. Newer statues tend to be seated on higher stools.

Some *Gouandousou* statues depict a belt-like chain of diamond shaped forms around the upper thighs and pubic area. Informants who were not very knowledgeable saw in this nothing more than a post-partum belt once worn by Bambara women. Post-partum necklaces of fragrant roots are still commonly worn by Bambara women. Knowledgeable informants said that this belt-like design depicted the scales of a snake. Some were more specific and said that the scales were those of the python, which symbolized progressive creation.

Gouantigui Statues

These statues, similar in size to *Gouandousou* ones, depict standing men, men on horseback or seated men. The latter are relatively rare. The standing figures frequently hold a knife pointed upwards or an animal horn. The mounted figures have a knife or arrowhead held up in one hand and thrust forward. These statues often depict tresses and the *bamada* hat, with or without talismans. Most statues fall within the height range of 35 to 45 inches and have patinas as described above for the *Gouandousou* statues. The male statues are referred to as *Gouantigui* (chief of the *Gouan*). In northern areas, *Gouantigui* statues are said to symbolize *Ndomadyiri*, the divine blacksmith. The knives and arrowheads held by these statues are said by some to symbolize the smith's iron. Others say these weapons symbolize power and rank. Some *Gouantigui* statues are depicted holding a horn, the kind of horn used for the storage of herbal medicines. This symbolizes *Ndomadyiri's* role as the master healer.

In those areas where *Gouandousou* is seen as a legendary ancestor, *Gouantigui* is perceived as her husband. Although of high rank, his powers are said to have been less than hers. Yet they complemented hers, because they were of a different nature. This analysis of *Gouantigui*, offered by several informants, struck me as an attempt by a male dominated society to deal with the thorny issue posed by a legend whose central theme is female supremacy.

As already mentioned, some informants view *Gouantigui* as symbolizing a collectivity of male ancestors. One informant interestingly perceived *Gouantigui* as symbolizing the first *Dyo Sia.*

Gouan Nyeni Statues

A third statue, that was housed with the other two, or with the *Gouandousou* when it was housed alone was that of a standing female figure without a child. Statues of this kind are called *Gouan Nyeni* (little girl *Gouan*). The color and patina of these statues are similar to those of the other two. They vary in height from about 35 to 45 inches and are of the same style as the statues with which they were housed. Sometimes there was more than one *Gouan Nyeni* statue in a shrine. Some are depicted holding their arms upward in front, touching their breasts while others have their arms down along their sides or upraised, holding a vessel. The posture of uplifted arms with hands on the breasts is also found in some seated *Gouandousou* statues without children. Some of the standing statues are depicted with pregnant abdomens.

The obvious question arises as to the differentiation of seated female *Gouan* statues without children. Are they *Gouandousou* or *Gouan Nyeni* statues? Many informants state they are *Gouandousou* statues, the posture of sitting being the differentiating architectonic characteristic. The validity of this interpretation is questionable, however.

Many informants today, including some of Bamako's African art dealers, put forth the view, also stated by Ezra, that the *Gouan Nyeni* statues represent attendants.[15] Al-

though this interpretation might be accurate, it seems to be an attempt to explain these statues in contemporary contextual terms, employing a logic that seems reasonable to both westerners and westernized Africans. A number of knowlegeable *Dyo Sia* in all areas where the *Gouan* existed do not agree with the interpretation. They relate that *Gouan Nyeni* represents earlier phases of *Gouandousou's* life. And thus by extension of meaning, these statues depict woman's ideal temporal progress from pre-marital youth, through pregnancy to motherhood. In their final analysis, therefore, all of these statues symbolize the various stages of *Gouandousou's* life, desired by most ancient Bambara women.

Dyonyeni Statues

A number of *Dyo* groups used small wooden statues during their rituals, often referred to by informants as *Dyonyeni.* The functional context of statues of this genre used by *N'Kenie* groups has already been discussed above. Similar statues were also used by *N'Tokofa* and *Duga* groups. In general they measure from about 18 inches to 21 inches in height. Significantly, they are stylistically quite distinct from the large *Gouan* statues just discussed. Their architectonics are in the main identical to those of most Bambara sculpture emphasizing abstract features in contrast to *Gouan* statues which are remarkable for their naturalistic ones. However, like many *Gouan* statues, they often depict a head crest that represents a rainbow, symbol of God's presence and the site of the celestial *bana* tree.

There is much that is different in the architectonics of *Gouan* and *Dyonyeni* statues, a finding that arouses inquiry and raises the possibility that these two groups of statues represent separate sculptural traditions. The smaller *Dyonyeni* statues appear to be much newer than many of the *Gouan* statues, a fact plausibly explained by informants. They point out that *Dyonyeni* statues were subjected to vigorous physical use compared to *Gouan* statues. They were transported long distances, danced with and placed on the dance arena during ritual performances. High damage rates meant that new statues had to be made at frequent intervals. By comparison, the large *Gouan* statues were exposed to few breakage or damage risks and were passed on from one generation to the next. Thus it is possible to conclude from this evidence that both statue types were the products of the same sculptural tradition. The *Gouan* statues reflect the styles of this tradition at a much earlier period, while the *Dyonyeni* are later forms whose styles might also reflect the influences of other Bambara sculptural traditions.

Thematically *Dyonyeni* statues usually portray women, although some depict hemaphrodites. These latter are said to symbolize the masculine role women assume in the *Dyo* society. Rarely female *Dyo* initiates carried sculpted male statues of the same size and style as the others, but possessing different sculptural details. A number of statues possess legs, although in some the torso terminates in a pole with a broad round base. This latter construction was extremely pragmatic as it made for easy handling during rituals. It also made it possible to place the statue upright on the ground of the dance arena. Paques reported that small wooden statues were used by the *N'Kenie* groups and that they lacked both arms and legs.

Dyonyeni statues were often decorated with masses of small colorful beads and frequently dressed in cache-sex aprons. In addition they were decorated with ear rings and sometimes with a cloth band around the upper forehead. The latter was also used on twin statues (*flanitokele*). Some statues portray the rainbow head crest. Although this crest was unique in the costumes of some *N'Kenie* and *Gouan* members, it appears on the statues used by many *Dyo* groups. Some *Dyonyeni,* however, do not exhibit the rainbow head crest. But the recurrent appearance of the rainbow crest theme in both *Dyo* and *Gouan* statuary is one more piece of evidence pointing to the closeness of these two societies.

It is virtually impossible to group categorize *Dyonyeni* statues in western collections unless their ethographic contexts were documented in the field. Compounding the problem is the fact that *Kwore* society initiates used similar statues.

Other Large Statues

There are presently in western collections some large standing Bambara figures of the *Gouan* type, but which appear to be extremely old. One of these figures, now in the collection of the Metropolitan Museum of Art in New York City was aged dated by the Carbon-14 method and found to be 270 years old + 90 years.[16] Stylistically this statue bears a resemblance to *Gouan* statues in general in that it has rounded and naturalistic features compared to the angular and abstract characteristics of most known Bambara art. Yet one must exert extreme caution in definitively classifying this sculpture as a *Gouan* statue. Its contextual history can only be surmised, not proven. While it certainly could have been made for the *Gouan*, it is also possible that it was made for another cult, long extinct or one that was an antecedent of the *Gouan*. In either case it could also have been subsequently used by the *Gouan*, much the same as the Dogon used Tellem sculpture that they found in burial caves. The fact that these older statues share many stylistic features with more recent *Gouan* sculptures, features not found in the mainstream of Bambara art, speaks for probable identical geographical origins. Thematic and stylistic similarities are also strong evidence for all of these statues being part of the same sculptural tradition, spanning many years.

The Production of Copies of *Gouan* Statuary

The excitement created by *Gouan* statues among European and American collectors and dealers in the late 1950's and early 1960's was transmitted to Bamako's Moslem African art dealers in due course. This excitement translated into a willingness to pay relatively large sums for more statues. Bamako's dealers responded to this increased demand in two ways. First they intensified their field efforts in order to find and bring out additional statues. And secondly they had statues faithfully copied and artificially patinated. The first effort had limited success because there were only a certain number of statues in villages and in some cases *Dyo Sia* put up significant defenses to protect them. In one village in the Dioila cercle, the *Gouan* statues were placed in a deep dry well for safe keeping.

Copies were first commissioned from among local blacksmiths. But these were generally quite new in appearance and did not go over well with European dealers. In the mid-1960's one Bamako dealer, who was a well-educated and well-traveled man, came to realize that he could not depend on the abilities of rural blacksmiths to faithfully reproduce authentic objects. Therefore, he set up his own workshop in the Djikoroni quarter of Bamako and hired blacksmiths who primarily produced Tellem statuary under his direct supervision from books and catalogues he had obtained on his trips to Europe. He experimented with a number of techniques for creating encrustation patinas. The two commonest ones he used were cement into which millet chaff was mixed and liquid gum arabic to which sand and millet chaff were added. The patinas created by both these techniques were indeed impressive. Authentic statues were copied directly whenever possible, and limbs or parts intentionally broken off if necessary and the stumps aged by placement in termite mounds. About two weeks of such placement results in the surface tracking frequently seen in old pieces.

A number of other dealers, as well as this one, made duplicates of *Gouan* statues. But unlike him, they tended to mass produce them, resulting in poor quality sculptures, easily identified as fakes. He on the other hand made and aged several *Gouandousou* statues a year. Yet, even these carefully sculpted objects were never fully convincing to the expert eye. Once he commissioned a *Gouantigui* statue, a horseman, copied from Goldwater's *Bambara Sculpture From The Western Sudan*. Eventually he started producing enlarged versions and directed his black-

smiths to produce stylistic features known to please Europeans. These statues sold extremely well, better in fact than his earlier more conforming fakes and the authentic ones he had purchased in the bush. Both of his categories of fakes are now in private and museum collections.

By the early 1970's *Gouandousou* statues were being mass produced from Bamako to San and stood in rows in souks in Abidjan, Dakar and Bamako. *Gouantigui* and *Gouan Nyeni* statues were never mass produced to the same degree, having far less appeal to Western buyers. In fact the Djikoroni workshop only rarely produced these other *Gouan* statues.

Summary

Both the *Dyo* and the *Gouan* were societies whose limited geographic distribution in a remote part of Bambara land kept them hidden from western outsiders until that point in time when they were on the verge of extinction. Although there is much that we know about these societies, there is also a great deal that remains a mystery. Unlike most other religious and judicial Bambara societies, these two escaped careful scrutiny while still in flower. What we do know consists of observations gathered at dusk so to speak and the whispered memories of old men and women who were society participants in their youth. It is easy to succumb to the temptation of deducing a contextual world from the silent testimony of stylistic and thematic architectonics. Those who do so produce stories whose current vocabulary and technical terminology have a certain appeal to contemporary western logic. But these stories cannot really tell us what actually happened nor do they have an enduring capacity to convince. The sculptures of the *Dyo* and *Gouan* are as the ancient Bambara would have them, They speak to those who know their spiritual language. But for those who do not understand this language, they represent perfection in communication, which is silence.

References

Introduction

1. Imperato, P.J., *African Folk Medicine: Practices and Beliefs of the Bambara and Other Peoples,* Baltimore York Press, 1977, p. 11

2. Delafosse, M. *Haut-Senegal – Niger,* Paris, Larose, 1912, Vol. 1, p. 286.

3. Ibid. Vol. 2, pp. 288-290.

4. Ibid. p. 317.

5. Paques, V. Bouffons Sacres du Cerele de Bougouni (Soudan Francais) *Journal de la Societe des Africanistes,* 24:63-110, 1954.

6. Imperato, P.J., *The Cultural Heritage of Africa,* Chanute, Kansas, Safari Museum Press, 1974, p. 27.

Chapter 1

1. Zahan D. *Societes d'Initiation Bambara: Le N'Domo, Le Kore,* Paris, Mouton, 1960.

2. Cisse, Y. et Dieterlen, G., *Les Fondements de la Societe d'Initiation du Komo,* Paris, Mouton, 1972.

3. Henry J., *L'Ame d'un Peuple Africain, Les Bambara,* Paris, Picard, 1920.

4. McNaughton, P.R., *Secret Sculptures of Komo,* Philadelphia, Institute For The Study of Human Issues, 1979.

5. Monteil, C., *Les Bambara de Segou et du Kaarta,* Paris, Larose, 1924.

6. Tauxier, L., *La Religion Bambara,* Paris, Librairie Orientaliste Paul Geuthner, 1927.

7. Travele, M., Le Komo ou Koma, *Outre-Mer,* 1:127-150, 1929.

8. Imperato, P.J., The Dance of the Tyi Wara, *African Arts,* IV, 1:8-13, 71-80, 1970.

9. Zahan, D., *Antilopes du Soleil: Arts et Rites Agraires d'Afrique Noire,* Vienna, A. Schendl, 1980.

10. Monteil, op. cit. pp. 234-287.

11. Tauxier, op. cit. pp. 303-309.

12. de Zeltner, R.P., Le Culte de Nama au Soudan, *Bulletin et Memoires de la Societe d'Anthropologie de Paris,* 1:361-362, 1910.

13. Henry, op. cit. pp. 95-96, 114.

14. Paques, V. *Les Bambara,* Paris, Presses Universitaires de France, 1954, p. 86.

15. Imperato, P.J., The Role of Women in Traditional Healing Among The Bambara of Mali, *Transactions of the Royal Society of Tropical Medicine and Hygiene,* 75, 6:766-770, 1981.

16. McNaughton, op. cit., p. 3.

17. Zahan, op. cit., *Societies d'Initiation,* pp. 131-135.

18. Mage, E., *Voyage dans le Soudan Occidental* (Senegambie-Niger), 1863-1866, Paris, Librairie Hachette, 1968.

19. Delafosse, M., *Haut-Senegal-Niger,* Tome II, *L'Histoire,* Paris, 1912, p. 318.

20. Tauxier, op. cit. p. 300.

21. Ibid. p. 301.

22. Ibid.

23. Ibid.

24. Ibid. p. 281.

25. Ibid. p. 301.

26. Dieterlen, G. *Essai Sur La Religion Bambara,* Paris, Presses Universitaires de France, 1951, p. 154.

27. Paques, V., Les Samake, *Bulletin de l'IFAN,* B, 18:369-390, 1956.

28. McNaughton, op. cit. pp. 7-9.

29. Ibid. p. 7.

Chapter 2

1. Balesi, C.J., *From Adversaries To Comrades In Arms: West Africans And The French Military, 1855-1918,* Waltham, Mass., Crossroads Press, 1979.

2. Zahan, D., *Societes d'Initiation Bambara: Le N'Domo, Le Kore,* Paris, Mouton, 1960, p. 134.

3. Ibid.

4. Henry, J., *L'Ame d'un Peuple Africain,* Les Bambara, Paris, Picard, 1910, p. 146.

5. Tauxier, L., *La Religion Bambara,* Paris, Librairie Orientaliste, Paul Guethner, 1927, p. 329.

6. Paques, V., Buffons Sacres du Cercle de Bougouni (Soudan Francais), *Journal de la Societe des Africanistes,* 24:63-110, 1954.

7. Imperato, P.J., *The Cultural Heritage of Africa,* Chanute, Kansas, Safari Museum Press, 1974, p. 27.

8. Ezra K., Mother and Child, and Female Figure, in *For Spirits and Kings, African Art from the Paul and Ruth Tishman Collection,* edited by S. Vogel, New York, The Metropolitan Museum of Art, 1981, pp. 26-27.

9. Ibid.

10. Paques, op. cit. Bouffons Sacres, p. 64.

11. Ibid. p. 65.

12. Ibid.

Chapter 3

1. Zahan, D., *La Dialectique du Verbe Chez les Bambara,* Paris, Mouton, 1963, pp. 116-120.

2. Paques, V., Bouffons Sacres du Cercle de Bougouni (Soudan Francais), *Journal de la Societe des Africanistes,* 24:63-110, 1954.

3. Ibid.

4. Zahan, D., *The Bambara,* Leiden, E.J. Brill, 1974, pp. 1-6.

5. de Ganay, S., Aspects de Mythologie et de Symbolique Bambara, *Journal de Psychologie Normal et Patho-logique,* 2:184, 1949.

Chapter 4

1. Paques, V., Bouffons Sacres du Cerele de Bougouni (Soudan Francais) *Journal de la Societe des Africanistes,* 1954, p. 79.

2. Ibid.

3. Ibid.

4. Ibid.

5. Ibid., p. 80.

6. Ibid. p. 79.

7. Ibid., p. 81.

8. Ibid.

9. Delafosse, M., Au Sujet des Cavernes Artificielles Recement Decouvertes dans le Cercle de Bougouni, *Revue d'Ethnographie et de Sociologie,* 248-251, 1913.

10. Paques, op. cit., pp. 82-87.

11. Ibid. p. 87.

12. Ibid.

13. Ibid.

14. Ibid. p. 88.

15. Ibid. p. 89.

16. Malle, Brahima, Personal Communication, Kinian, May, 1970.

17. Paques, op. cit., p. 90.

18. Ezra, K., Female Figure, in *For Spirits and Kings, African Art from the Paul and Ruth Tishman Collection,* edited by S. Vogel, New York, The Metropolitan Museum of Art, 1981, p. 27.

19. Malle, Brahima, op. cit.

20. Kolekele, N'Tyi, Personal Communications, Dioila, April 1974.

21. Paques, op. cit., p. 91.

22. Fall, Gassou, Personal Communication, Massigui, June, 1968.

23. Paques, op cit., pp. 93-107.

24. Ibid. p. 100-102.

25. Ibid. p. 101.

26. Ibid. p. 95.

27. Ibid.

28. Ibid. p. 96.

29. Ibid.

30. Ibid. p. 97.

31. Ibid. p. 73.

32. Imperato, P.J., *African Folk Medicine: Practices and Beliefs of the Bambara and Other Peoples,* Baltimore, York Press, 1977, p. 36.

33. Imperato, P.J., Door Locks of the Bamana of Mali, *African Arts,* V, 3:52-56, 1972.

34. Paques, op. cit., p. 108.

35. Ibid. p. 105.

36. Ibid.

37. Ibid.

38. Ibid.

39. Imperato, P.J. The Role of Women In Traditional Healing Among The Bambara of Mali, *Transactions of The Royal Society of Tropical Medicine and Hygiene,* 75, 6:766-770, 1981.

40. MacCormack, C.P., Health, Fertility and Birth In Moyamba District, Sierra Leone, in *The Ethnography of Fertility and Birth,* edited by C.P. MacCormack, London, Academic Press, 1982, pp. 115-139.

41. Glaze, A.J., *Art and Death In A Senufo Village,* Bloomington, Indiana, Indiana University Press, 1981, p. 87.

42. Henry, J., *L'Ame d'un Peuple Africain, Les Bambara,* Paris, Picard, 1910, pp. 95-96, 114.

43. Ibid.

44. Ibid.

45. Ibid.

46. Ibid.

47. Ibid.

48. Ibid.

49. Ibid.

50. Ibid.

51. Ezra, K., Mother and Child, in *For Spirits and Kings, African Art From the Paul and Ruth Tishman Collection,* edited by S. Vogel, New York, The Metropolitan Museum of Art, 1981, p. 26.

52. Ezra, K., Female Figure, in *For Spirit and Kings, African Art from the Paul and Ruth Tishman Collection,* edited by S. Vogel, New York, The Metropolitan Museum of Art, 1981, p. 27.

53. Ibid.

Chapter 5

1. Paques, V., Les Samake, *Bulletin de l'IFAN,* XVIII, Series B, 3-4: 369-390, 1956.

2. Zahan, D., Antilopes, du *Soleil, Arts et Rites Agraires d'Afrique Noire,* Vienna, A. Schendl, 1980, pp. 124-125.

3. Ibid.

4. Paques, V., Bouffons Sacres du Cerele de Bougouni (Soudan Francais) *Journal de la Societe des Africanistes,* 24:63-110, 1954.

5. Zahan, op. cit., *Antilopes du Soleil,* pp. 123-124.

6. Sylla, Mamadou, Personal Communication, Bamako, June 1970.

7. Diabete, Moussa, Personal Communication, Bamako, July, 1967.

8. Niono, Tiemoko, Personal Communication, Bamako, August, 1971.

9. Goldwater, R., *Bambara Sculpture From The Western Sudan,* New York, Museum of Primitive Art, 1960, p. 17.

10. Ibid.

11. Imperato, P.J., *The Cultural Heritage of Africa,* Chanute Kansas, Safari Museum Press, 1974, p. 27.

12. Ezra, K., Mother and Child, in *For Spirits and Kings, African Art from the Paul and Ruth Tishman Collection,* edited by S. Vogel, New York, The Metropolitan Museum of Art, 1981, p. 26.

13. Ezra, Female Figure, in *For Spirits and Kings, African Art from the Paul and Ruth Tishman Collection,* edited by S. Vogel, New York, The Metropolitan Museum of Art, 1981, p. 27.

14. Ezra, op. cit. Mother and Child.

15. Ezra, op. cit., Female Figure, p. 27.

16. Northern T., The African Collection At The Museum of Primitive Art, *African Arts,* V., 1:20-27, 1971.

PHOTOGRAPHIC CREDITS

Professor Viviana Paques: Figures 8-15

Mrs. Marli Shamir: Figures 22-25

The Metropolitan Museum of Art. The Michael C. Rockefeller Memorial Collection: Figures 5-7, 19-21, 27, 34-35.

Author: Figures 1-4, 16-18, 26, 28-33 and Cover.

OBJECTS DEPICTED

The Metropolitan Museum of Art. The Michael C. Rockefeller Memorial Collection: Figures 5-7, 19-21, 27, 34-35.

The Dr. and Mrs. Pascal James Imperato Collection: Figures 16-18, 22-26, 28-33 and Cover.